# GO NAKED

Best Wishes

# GO NAKED

REVEALING
THE SECRETS OF
SUCCESSFUL SELLING

# MICHAEL SMITH

# R3THINK PRESS

First published in 2014 by Rethink Press (www.rethinkpress.com)

Illustrations by John Montgomery

Author Photograph by Darren Garwood Photography

*For Andrea*

# PRAISE

A fabulous read! Great insights into how to build relationships and be more successful in sales without selling. Michael really shows us how to 'GO NAKED'!

SHAA WASMUND, ENTREPRENEUR AND AUTHOR OF
#1 BEST SELLER, *STOP TALKING, START DOING*

In Michael Smith's book, *GO NAKED*, you're going to discover why honesty, authenticity and a relentless service-orientation are the keys to building real relationships and outselling the competition in the new economy.

JAMIE SMART, AUTHOR OF #1 BEST SELLER,
*CLARITY: CLEAR MIND, BETTER PERFORMANCE, BIGGER RESULTS*

*GO NAKED* is a must-read for anyone in business. No matter what your job title, you are in sales and this book will show you how exactly how to stand out in your industry.

JACQUELINE BIGGS, INTERNATIONAL
BEST-SELLING AUTHOR, *MARKETING TO WIN*

Michael Smith's *GO NAKED* exposes everything you need to know about how to sell and how not to sell. From the beginning, he dispels myths and archaic ways of thinking, replacing outdated high-pressure, pump-and-dump techniques with fresh insights on building win-win relationships that last for a lifetime. Michael has a unique ability to break down complex topics into digestible chunks while also helping the reader zoom out to see and process the big picture. This book is a timely read for anyone in business looking to create lifelong clients who are also raving fans.

ISAIAH HANKEL, AUTHOR, *BLACK HOLE FOCUS*

*GO NAKED* is the very essence of what it means to put the customer at the centre of all thinking. It strips away the perceived need for layers of tricks and tips and reiterates the fundamental fact, applicable to us all, that we only have our reputation. *GO NAKED* causes us to think deeply about how to build and safeguard that reputation and truly be accepted as a trusted advisor by the customer.

RICHARD BEAUMONT, EMEA SALES TRAINING MANAGER

# CONTENTS

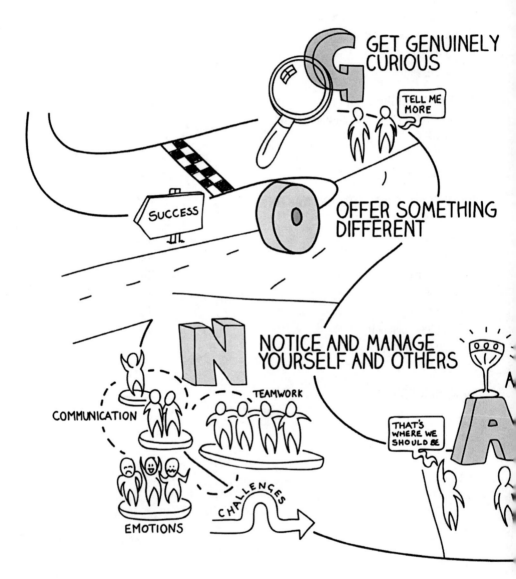

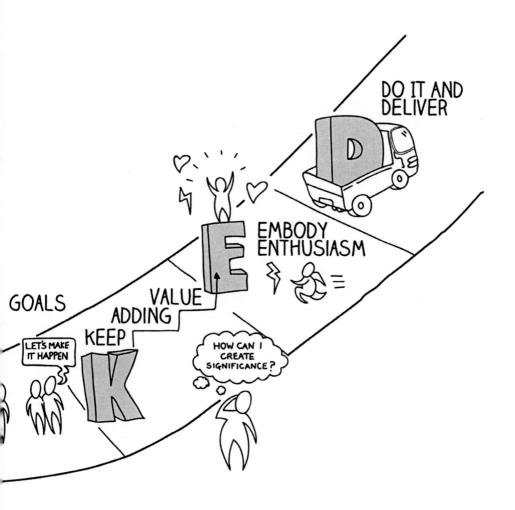

# THAT FEELING

*The greatest risk for most of us in life*
*isn't that our aim is too high and we miss,*
*but that it's too low and we achieve it.*
MICHELANGELO, ARTIST, ARCHITECT AND POET

Back when I was in high school, I turned up to a gym lesson and, as we always did, began the ritual of getting ready for the lesson. The uniform at that time was a particularly unflattering white t-shirt and a pair of silky black shorts.

I'm sure you can picture the scene – organised chaos probably describes it – and, through the noise and hurry, I noticed a friend of mine standing looking into his bag, appearing anxious and concerned. He had forgotten his kit.

I walked over to him and offered to help. We asked around to see if anyone had any spare kit – they didn't – and so he went to see the teacher to explain what had happened. Expecting a reprieve from the lesson, my friend was taken aback as the teacher turned and said, 'Don't worry, you can just do it in your underwear!'

I was shocked. I couldn't believe what was happening. In that moment, my concern for my friend evaporated and my natural instinct kicked in as I shot over to my bag to check that all my kit was in there – there was no way I was going to risk doing the lesson in my underwear.

Now, had it been me I probably would have just gone home and I certainly wouldn't have done the class. My friend, however, strode into the gym with all the confidence in the world. And whilst at first all of the kids in there laughed, by the end of the lesson he was the hero for having the courage and confidence to do the lesson almost naked.

For some time afterwards I would often have a dream of turning up at gym class naked.

Did you ever have a dream during which you turned up to a party, to school or to work… naked?

In that split second when you woke up, how did you feel?

*Scared? Excited? Vulnerable?*

These are the same feelings we get when we step out of our comfort zone and take risks – and the most successful people do this every day. It's what drives them. It's what sets them apart from the rest. It's what makes them successful.

When you lay yourself bare, when you strip away superfluous behaviour, when you remove limiting beliefs, then in doing so, you open up a world of possibilities. It becomes easier to communicate and easier to build relationships because you demonstrate more of the authentic person you really are.

We all go through times when we feel we need to put up barriers or a façade in the hope that we become more credible, more believable, more worthy, more important. But the truth is that, in building relationships of any sort, these behaviours don't contribute to the successful development of long-lasting relationships. At best, they hinder it and, at worst, they create relationships built on weak foundations that have no long-term sustainability.

Successful selling, relationship development and influencing are all about the manner in which we communicate. Let's face it, we all have to do this every day of our lives, whether personally or professionally. And the most successful people, the most successful communicators, influencers and relationship builders, are able to do so because they lay themselves bare.

Fortunately there is a pattern – a set of principles – and at its heart is the awareness for the need to strip away behaviour which doesn't contribute to success. Successful people remove the unnecessary layers, let go of limiting beliefs and are prepared to leave themselves open and vulnerable. They *GO NAKED*.

# LIFE IS ALL ABOUT RELATIONSHIPS

*If you want to make a real difference in people's lives, your commitment to giving them value has to outweigh your craving for their approval.*
JAMIE SMART, AUTHOR, SPEAKER AND COACH

Life is all about relationships. Whether we succeed or fail will ultimately be determined by the number of quality relationships we have. And no one is exempt from this. Whether you are in school or university; looking for work or in work; in music, the arts, sport or business; climbing the corporate ladder or setting out on your own, it is relationships and the strength of those relationships which matter and make the difference.

## PICTURE THE SCENE

A friend of yours is sitting in front of you. He's looking for a job, but it's tough out there at the moment and he's had no luck. You ask him what he's been doing to change his fortune and he tells you that he's been sending his CV to countless companies. 'It's so demoralising,' he tells you – and you bet it is. Ask him what else he's done to further his chances and he tells you he's been searching the internet for hours looking for companies who are recruiting, but there's just nothing out there. 'It's just so miserable trawling the internet for hours,' he tells you – and you couldn't agree more. Ask him if there's anything else he's tried and he tells you there isn't much more he can do. 'The jobs go to friends of friends,' he proclaims, and that 'it's all about who you know, not what you know.' You agree that there's probably some truth in that. Ask him what more he could be doing to get the job he wants and he looks blank. 'What more *can* I do?' he asks in return.

A colleague of yours sits down for coffee with you. She's been passed over for promotion and just can't understand why. You ask her what went wrong and she doesn't know. She completed her application letter in time, turned up at the interview and performed well, she even had a letter of recommendation from her boss. 'It's just not fair,' she tells you – and you agree it's not. Ask her what she'll do differently next time to make sure the same doesn't happen again and she tells you, 'Nothing.' That she doesn't know what more she can do. Ask her why she believes the other person got the job ahead of her and she's convinced it's the same old story – that it was probably a *fait accompli* from the start. You agree she's probably right.

A guy you used to work with has recently set up his own business and you bump into him in the local Starbucks. He's feeling pretty down at the moment – none of his old clients moved with him when he left. Running his own business is 'far harder than I imagined,' he tells you – you bet it is. You ask him what he's been doing to try and drive a change and get things moving. He says he's spent hours emailing old clients asking for business, but of course 'the economy is bad at the moment and it's just so depressing – no reply after no reply.' You can only imagine. You ask him what's next and he tells you he's out of ideas. It's been three months and he'll probably just have to try and get his old job back. 'At least I was safe there,' he tells you. You wonder whether he'll get close to getting his old job back and even if he does, *how* safe would he actually be?

## PLAYING WITH THE MAJORITY

Getting a new job – a job you really want – in a competitive environment is tough. There are a lot of bright, well qualified people out there with relevant experience. However, there are also a lot of less intelligent, less qualified people out there with only limited experience. But guess what? The majority are all doing the same thing. They're submitting their CVs and writing splendid cover letters, getting in line with everyone else. They go to monster.com and become one of the 63 million people looking for a job every month. No wonder it's hard.

Getting the promotion to the job you really want is equally challenging. Standing out from the crowd without leaving a cast of fallen colleagues behind isn't easy and requires you to buck corporate wisdom. Because that's what the majority are doing – playing a game of 'one-upmanship' with the person next to them; sending in their application and 'getting in line'. Yes, it's crowded out there and corporate life can at times feel like the opening scenes to *Saving Private Ryan*. Being the best employee, the best sales person, or the best marketer in the business is hard. But take a look at the company awards dinner. All too often, it's the same person or small group of people who win, year after year.

And finally, starting anything new and succeeding, regardless of the project or venture, is a slog which requires dedication and persistence – to say nothing of the need for it to be better than what exists out there today. The problem is that the majority of new things out there aren't better than what's already out there. Most are equitable at best.

The truth is that we're all in sales now. Whatever your business, whatever your role – a key part, in fact the primary part which will determine success is to the extent to which you can create great relationships.

## WHAT'S THE GOOD NEWS?

There are three types of people. 'Lost Souls', 'the Majority' and 'Stars'. The good news is that the 'lost souls' out there are few and far between: individuals and businesses so incapable of doing something different occupy only a relatively small proportion of the population, so the chances of falling into that group are small.

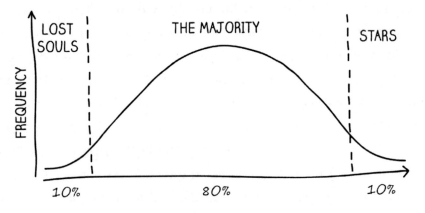

Depending on your view point, the fact that 'the majority' occupies such a large proportion of the curve is either bad or good news. Bad news if your mindset is close to those individuals referenced in the familiar stories above; good news, however, if you see the crowded majority as an opportunity to position yourself differently and to break out from the rest. Those people, the top 10 percent, are the 'stars', the differentiators, the ones on stage at the company awards dinner and the ones who stand out from the crowd. They're a small but powerful group – the ones who get the job or promotion they want, move from successful project to successful venture and who are amongst the top performers in their organisation.

## WHAT DO THE 'STARS' DO DIFFERENTLY?

If they're looking for a job, they don't join the majority. They don't send CVs and cover letters in on spec; they don't join the millions queuing virtually on line at monster.com; and they don't search aimlessly without clarity and focus. They understand that it's personal connections that matter and the value of a quality network and relationships. They find someone in the same industry or company they want to work in. If they don't know someone directly, they find someone who knows someone. They spend time with them and, for the price of a cup of coffee, ask them for their help – not in getting a job directly, but in helping them understand what it takes to get a job and succeed. They ask for a referral and they take whatever advice or guidance comes their way before determining what may or may not work for them – usually by giving it a go.

If they want progression or a promotion, they don't stand in line waiting with the majority for 'fairness' but they set their vision out early. And, critically, they don't just focus on the next job but beyond that role to the n+1 job – the one after the next one – and develop their skillset and network to support that goal. They invest in themselves, they put themselves in front of the right people and they create an opportunity. And when that opportunity arrives, they grab it with both hands.

If they're in sales – and everyone is to some extent – they realise that the biggest difference between them and 'the majority' is their mindset. That they are the ones in control of their business – that despite external circumstances they can adapt their offering in a way that resonates with their customers. They have relationships that stand the test of time and the foresight to create new opportunities long before others have realised there's a need. They use a series of simple but proven principles and are never short of ideas.

And when they start something new – a project or venture – they look for a gap, a niche, and they make sure that it's aligned with their capabilities. Then they go after it, with verve and gusto. They go into it with their eyes wide open and a plan to accompany it. They accept there may be some highs and lows, but they see an end point which they keep fixated on. They get good people around them and aren't afraid to ask for help. They're proactive and committed to action with purpose rather than the worthless option of low quality activity for the sake of it.

For 'the majority' who stand and point at 'the stars' and tell tales of woe; who talk of fairness (or lack thereof); who point to the conditions on the playing field as the reason for their performance whilst others around them on the same field win; who, rather than try something new for fear of failure, stand in the perceived safety of the line; and who don't ask for help or invest in themselves it will remain hard if not impossible.

This is a book about relationships: about how to develop better, stronger, deeper relationships with people, and how to create significance in business life or personal life.

It's also a book about the majority, or actually about how to stand out from the majority. It's a book about how to become one of the 'stars', one of the top 10 percent.

Because being in the top 10 percent is tough – that's why it's reserved for the best. But it doesn't have to be impossible; in fact it's not. It's just reserved for those who step out of line, away from the majority and strip away the low quality think-ing and limiting beliefs that hold many people back.

## WHY DO SO MANY PEOPLE FALL INTO 'THE MAJORITY'?

There is a fundamental issue with our conventional understanding of sales.

In the traditional approach to selling, conventional wisdom teaches us to identify customers' needs through a series of funnelled questions and match those identified needs to our relevant *features and benefits* (the *transaction*). The features are the particular element of the product or service which is most suited to them, and the benefit is the 'what's in it for them' or 'what does that mean to them'.

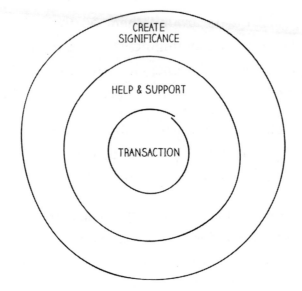

Once needs have been established, features and benefits matched, the next step is to agree a mutually beneficial way forward of which one positive outcome is a sale, in whatever form it takes. After the sale is complete the *customer support* element starts. We find ways to provide a service or support mechanism to ensure the use of our product or service – hence the term 'after sales service'. (We *help and support*)

If we're lucky, our relationship develops through the sales process and we may progress to a position as being seen as a *valued or trusted advisor* by the customer.

This is what I would term the 'traditional' model of selling:

1. Sell based on features and benefits
2. Provide after sales support or service
3. Become (if lucky) a valued or trusted advisor

## THE ROUTE TO GREAT RELATIONSHIPS

It is in the top right-hand corner of this diagram where we (as relationship builders, influencers or sales people) are able to create the greatest amount of value, and where the other person – whether customers or otherwise – generate the greatest level of contribution.

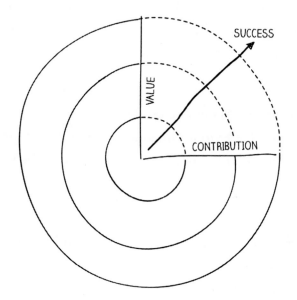

In business, this is where you get repeat business, can charge more for your products or services, and sell additional or complementary products or services. It's where the customer perceives a greater level of value being transferred to them and where the customer generates more sales and profit for the company or individual. In your personal life, this is the area where you get the most from your relationships. These are the people who you add value to but who also contribute greatly to your life.

And importantly, regardless of the context, this is the area in which you step away from the majority.

In the traditional model of selling, the relationship is built on the foundations of a transaction, on the feature-benefit sell. The help and support, and the journey to becoming a valued or trusted advisor where the relationship is most fruitful for everyone involved, becomes secondary. There is a lag and many business and sales people will admit that they don't get there. It is the promised-land – the area we all strive to operate in – but the one that for most individuals is never quite achieved because we're too focused on the transaction.

It is that way, not because of a lack of ability on the part of the individual or the sales person, but because of where the focus lies; on the way in which we approach the relationship, primarily on the transaction – feature-benefit sale – rather than the individual.

## FLIP IT

The way to step away from the majority and the way to overcome these issues are to invert the traditional selling model, to flip it. This means to forget yourself and to focus first on creating significance, then to offer help and support so that finally the transactional element, or the feature-benefit, becomes a *fait accompli*. It just becomes a matter of course and an inevitable result of an early focus on the other person, rather than focusing first on the features of the product or service. It is a focus away from the transaction and a focus away from the initial idea of selling.

So let's take a look at this principle in a little more detail and provide some greater insight as to its application. After all, it's fine in theory, but how does this come to life?

## START BY CREATING SIGNIFICANCE

When you build a relationship, a really great relationship, there are certain elements that are both integral to and consistent in what makes a successful relationship.

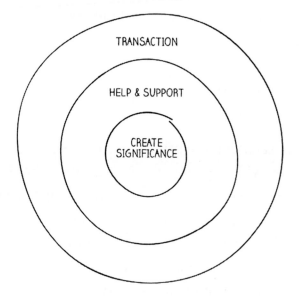

If we can focus first on building and amplifying these areas, then the traditional model inverts. Our primary goal becomes to create value and significance for the other person; we shift the focus away from us and our agenda and instead make it all about others.

In business and sales, we can improve the experience our customers have of working with us before moving on to the transactional part and the feature-benefit sale.

It's not exclusive to business. More generally, if we focus first on the other person and creating value and significance for them, we can mutually benefit from the help and support available to get more out of our relationships. And this is where

*GO NAKED* is centred – on first creating significance by adopting seven principles, which are to:

- Get Genuinely Curious
- Offer Something Different
- Notice and Manage Yourself and Others
- Agree Goals
- Keep Adding Value
- Embody Enthusiasm
- Do It And Deliver

We'll explore each of these principles in detail, but none of them should be viewed independently. Instead they should be seen a series of interconnecting points on a grid, each one linked with the other, bound together by a mindset and an approach which strips away the layers of conventional wisdom that don't contribute to success. This mindset requires us to be authentic and honest, to take action and take risks, to ask for help without fear of rejection, and to show humility. It requires us to *GO NAKED*.

In discussing what it means to create significance for someone and to focus on being a trusted or valued advisor, in highlighting the areas which contribute to the development of these sorts of relationships, then we are starting to peel back the layers and understand what it actually means to *GO NAKED*.

This book will, if you allow it, help you develop ways to build stronger relationships with people so that whether you are selling yourself, a product or a service, you can step away from the majority and increase the chances of longer-term success.

Read on to find out how.

# GET GENUINELY CURIOUS

*I had no idea that being your authentic self could make me as rich as I've become. If I had, I'd have done it a lot earlier.*
OPRAH WINFREY, PRESENTER AND PRODUCER

*Understanding can overcome any situation, however mysterious or insurmountable it may appear to be.*
NORMAN VINCENT PEALE, MINISTER AND AUTHOR

The best relationships are those built on a desire to better understand the other person. But all too often, that simple principle is forgone in favour of an approach which is far more superficial and centered on the realisation of a predetermined agenda. Why? Because it means putting the other person first, and this, according to conventional wisdom, means that it may take more time to be successful.

Today, that's what the majority are doing.

They're driving their own agenda as quickly as possible, sometimes coated in an icing of friendliness and pleasantries but nonetheless lacking the desire to connect with people in an authentic way, which would benefit each person over the longer-term. And the reason you know that's what the majority are doing is because by definition, the majority is getting pretty average results.

## A BEAUTIFUL COMBINATION

Think of the people you meet who you find engaging and interesting. Many times, they're the people who took more of an interest in you than in trying to demonstrate how interesting they were. Give some thought to those people with whom you have the strongest relationships – family and close friends, for instance. What are some of the common denominators? Most likely they include openness, authenticity, interest and curiosity. It's no accident that these are the same principles which also make a great sales person.

If you look up the word 'Genuine', you'll see that it can be defined as *possessing the claimed or attributed character, quality, or origin; authentic; real*. If you are 'genuine', then, your behaviour is described by a powerful adjective which puts you ahead of the majority when it comes to building relationships with others.

The word 'curious' is derived from the Latin term *curiosus*, which means careful, diligent, attentive and inquisitive. When we think of someone as curious, we relate the term to inquisitive thinking, exploration, investigation and learning. And so as curiosity represents a desire for knowledge; people who are curious have a thirst for knowledge.

When you Get Genuinely Curious these two *
beautifully and their output is extremely power
erately and consciously strive to understand mor
other person first and make them central to your thin
an openness and willingness to engage with them.

This comes from a desire to truly understand the other pers
and their circumstances. To do so requires the confidence to
shift your focus away from you, onto the other person; to be
willing to stand authentic and show the real you; to take a
genuine interest in them – by listening actively to and responding to their words; and finally by giving people time.

This can be scary; it can certainly feel unusual. Accepting these
feelings and embracing them is the hallmark of being genuinely
curious, and the hallmark of those who stand out from the
majority and *GO NAKED*.

## CARE MORE ABOUT THE OTHER
## PERSON THAN YOU DO YOURSELF

Developing relationships is a two way process, however you
have to care more about the other person than you do about
yourself. To care more about the other person than you do yourself requires a shift in traditional thinking – because it's not
about you or what you need. Instead you're focused on the other
person, what they say and how you respond. You're forgoing
your own selfish desires to put the other person first. That's a
brave place to be because there's no roadmap, you have no idea
where the conversation will go and you have to be willing to

person, your agenda abandoned,

neeting or a sales call everyone
there with the aim of winning
That's obvious and would be

…emphasise that fact. You don't need
… with a list of scripted questions and you don't need
to force an agenda. Come the end of the meeting, the person or
persons sitting opposite you will either want to work with you
or they won't. They'll either want to buy from you or they
won't. They'll make a decision as to whether you are the best
person for them to work with at that time. And that's all there
is to it. It's really no more complicated than that.

But going in and trying to drive the conversation and agenda
based solely on you and what you want will limit your ability
to understand more about the other person and how best to
serve them, and thus reduce your chances of success.

The answer is to forget traditional thinking and forget pushing
your own agenda. Instead, focus on the other person – what
they want, what they need and what makes their world go
round. It means to ask them, 'What would need to happen
between now and the end of the meeting for you to think that
I/we are worth working with in the future?' And listening to
the answer, not knowing where it may take you.

Do you have that level of confidence?

Often our instinct when we meet someone is to tell them all about us, about our agenda, about what we want from the situation. Resist that urge. It's an urge born out of the desire to want to fill the gaps, to talk for the sake of talking, to appear interesting and because we think that it's a short cut to success.

Step back from the brink of making that mistake and instead re-focus your attention on the other person.

## WHAT ARE YOUR VALUES?

Ask this question in an interview and you can be sure that the answer will be 'integrity'. Follow that question up with another to ascertain exactly what is meant by integrity and you will often find that 'integrity' is defined as 'honesty'.

Integrity is multi-faceted but is primarily about demonstrating behaviours which are congruent with your values. For example, if one of your values is 'hard work', acting with integrity means your behaviour should reflect that value. In other words, you wouldn't expect someone with a stated value of 'hard work' to cut corners, only do half a job or the minimum required, and say that they were acting with integrity.

Honesty, though, is *part* of integrity – and that seems to confuse some people. You need to be honest with yourself as to whether your behaviour is a reflection of your values. Honesty is one component of integrity; another is authenticity – or, to put another way, being genuine.

# THE ANTIDOTE TO FAKE

Fake is all around us. Everywhere we look.

A recent review suggested that the criminal gain from counterfeiting in the UK was worth £1.3 billion every year. The products included in this sum included everything from luxury goods, toys, DVDs and CDs to power tools.

A recent YouGov survey found that 24 percent of adults have knowingly bought a fake DVD. The International Chamber of Commerce expects that by 2015 the value of counterfeit goods globally will exceed $1.7 trillion. That's over 2 percent of the world's total current economic output.

From products to groups, there are now a plethora of fake businesses out there and fake people to go with them – from fake online sites to Twitter accounts, all with the purpose of capturing your information and leveraging it for their gain.

Add to this our demand for more reality TV and it's easy to see why this adjusted version of reality, with the embellished personal stories and hyperbole leading to instant fame, is what has become our expected norm.

Yes, it's everywhere and, as a result of the increase in this 'culture of fake', it becomes easier for us – perhaps even the accepted or encouraged norm – to go through our days operating behind a façade, creating an adjusted version of 'us', ostensibly for the benefit of ourselves and others.

I've done this before. I'm sure you have too. But why?

## 1. Protection

Like a suit of armour, offering up an adjusted version of 'the real me' gives you protection.

> *'If they don't like me, that's ok. It's not the*
> *real me they're seeing anyway.'*

## 2. Acceptance

Most of us want to be liked and be accepted. We worry that being the 'real us' may put the chances of acceptance at risk and so we adjust our behaviour.

> *'If I behave more like X, I'm more likely to be accepted.'*

## 3. Promotion

We worry that the 'real us' wouldn't get *that* job, *that* offer, *that* position, *that* opportunity. So we put on a show more aligned with what we think the person or persons responsible for choosing are looking for.

What's ironic about this is that as a result of our adjusted behaviour we're unable to build the same connections with people that we potentially could, as we fail to understand the 'real them' and vice versa.

Eventually, though, we succeed or fail through our authenticity.

## THE RISK OF NOT BEING 'THE REAL YOU'

If an individual is in a position where they can no longer act authentically, the dissonance, or the lack of harmony between the person they are and the behaviour they exhibit becomes too great and they risk failure. (For example, individuals who are promoted from their peers to manage a team often feel they have to be a different person to the one they were previously, rather than accepting that they're the same person, with the same qualities, just in a different role.)

Put another way, we all have times when we are 'ourselves', when we feel safe in the knowledge that we can show the real us – and that authenticity is attractive. At other times we feel the need to present an adjusted version of this to other people. In the event that we spend too much time in a company or a role where we are the latter (where we aren't 'the real us'), then the chances of failure are also higher.

So what's the antidote to this?

To be authentic is to be genuine. And importantly, it's linked not only with how you connect with other people, but also how you connect with yourself.

That's important, so let me say it again.

> *Authenticity is linked not only with how you connect*
> *with other people, but also how you connect with yourself.*

The degree to which you want to be genuine and live with authenticity is up to you. But it is a choice and one you can decide to take. How you do so is personal. There's no formula, but there are a few things you can do to help others see the real you and to be comfortable in showing and being the real you.

Know what **YOUR VALUES** are.

What are the things that are most important to you? What are the things that drive your decision-making? Ensure you know what they are – write them down in a visible place – and look at them regularly. Ensure your behaviour is congruent with your values and take the time to explain them to people. They may not agree with them and they may not be the same as theirs, but they're more likely to understand you and the decisions you make because of it.

Tell **YOUR STORY.**

We've all got a story to tell, so tell it. Let people know about you, what makes you 'you', where you've come from and how you've ended up where you are today. If this makes you uncomfortable, that's ok. It means you're stretching your thinking and behaviour to new places. Go there and embrace it.

Be clear what **YOUR POSITION** is and where your boundaries lie.

People like security and comfort and they like to know where they stand. Be clear on what your position is – values are a part of this. Let people know where your boundaries are and when they've crossed them. Be consistent. Be fair.

Authenticity is a key component of building relationships – of business, of selling and of leadership – and it isn't reserved for an elite few, for world or corporate leaders, but for everyone who wants to make a difference. Everyone can be authentic.

When you're genuine, when you live with authenticity, you open up a world of possibilities. It becomes easier to communicate and easier to build relationships as you demonstrate more of the 'authentic you' and less of an adjusted version of someone you're trying to be. You can't fake it, nor should you try.

If you're open with others, you'll put them at ease. You'll remove barriers and allow them in turn to be more authentic with you.

## YOU HAVE TO GIVE PEOPLE TIME

Giving people time is critical to being curious about others. However, it's not an easy one for many people, especially in our results-orientated culture, so it's not for the fainthearted! It requires bravery and a willingness to slow things down and accept that some things just take time.

## TAKE TIME TO LISTEN

Active listening means exactly that. It is a behaviour that requires active participation. It is not sitting listening while your mind jumps around all the other things that co-exist in the recesses of your subconscious – the holiday you need to book, the shopping you need to pick up on the way home, what your next question may be; it is listening, understanding, processing and responding accordingly.

If anyone ever tells you that using a list of pre-determined questions is a good way to build any sort of relationships with anyone, they're wrong. It doesn't work. Because it breaks the flow and the links between what one person is saying and how the other person reacts, naturally, curiously.

# GIVE PEOPLE TIME TO ANSWER QUESTIONS

Ask yourself the following questions:

*How often do you ask someone a question and then answer it for them before they've even had a chance to answer?*

*How often does it happen to you?*

*How often do you finish someone else's sentence for them?*

*How often does it happen to you?*

*How often does someone pause, looking for the right word, and you 'find it' for them?*

*How often does it happen to you?*

## Getting the wrong idea

George and Sarah were both middle managers in a multi-national pharmaceutical company. They were together at a team meeting for a couple of days, and taking time away from the meeting to get a coffee and discuss the latest happenings within their respective teams.

Andy worked for Sarah and had done for a couple of years. He'd been a consistent performer over that time, always achieving his objectives and never giving Sarah any cause for concern. Until now.

It was strange, and had just come out of the blue. Over the last few weeks, he'd stopped calling Sarah as much. It had gone from almost every day to only once a week. She decided to tell the story to George.

'He's never given me any cause for concern,' said Sarah, 'so this was really odd behaviour from him. I decided to meet up with him to understand what was going on,' Sarah continued. 'We got together last Friday and when I asked him about it, he said...' Sarah paused.

'He's leaving!' George jumped in.

Sarah looked at him, stunned.

'No,' she said. 'Of course not. Whatever gave you that idea?'

'Well, I don't know,' said George apologetically. 'I just thought…'

'Well, anyway… we got together last Friday and when I asked him about it, he said that there was nothing at all wrong. He was trying to be a bit more independent and less of a burden to me. He said he knew I had my hands full with the trainees and wanted to leave me to it. We've agreed that's not necessary, that he can call as often as he likes, and since then things have returned to normal.'

## JUMPING INTO THE SPACE

Jumping into the space people leave when they talk is a common mistake which many of us make. We do it for various reasons: we do it because we're afraid or because we lack confidence; to try and show how much we know, or how much we thought we knew about what the other person was going to say; we do it to keep the pace of the conversation, and sometimes just because we're impatient and the silence is deafening!

But the next time you do any of the above, or someone does one of them to you while you're talking, take the time to notice it and the impact it has on the conversation.

When you ask someone a question, give them time to answer it – don't answer it for them.

When someone stops mid-sentence to think, don't just jump into the space – there isn't room in there for both of you!

When they pause to find the right word – don't find it for them. They know better than anyone what they wanted to say.

## ALLOW TIME TO THINK

All too often we ask a question or make a comment intended to provoke a response and then just keep talking, like some kind of uncontrollable force.

When you've asked a question…

Pause.

This isn't a race or a competition for who can say the most or say it the quickest. Be comfortable to leave the silence hanging. Let the other person think, process what they've just heard and assemble their thoughts.

And I'm not talking about a gap of a second or two; I'm talking about a real gap – five to ten seconds, to ensure that the other person has nothing more to say. Count them out in your mind.

By the same token, you need to give yourself time to think. Don't try and react immediately to what has been said. Be comfortable with the pause and the silence while you gather your thoughts as a truly reflective response.

Leaving a silence, especially during an important conversation, requires courage. In return, you're rewarded with a powerful tool.

## PROVIDE THE TIME TO MAKE DECISIONS

Everyone wants to win, and conventional wisdom tells us that we have to push for a decision. The problem with pushing for a decision is that you've traded something – you've traded the opportunity of time for a decision. In pushing someone for a decision, you are eroding the likelihood of them taking responsibility, and when someone trades their responsibility is it rarely a good thing.

Whilst you may get a quick win or sale by not giving someone time, that's all you're getting. So if you're in the business of quick sales and one-off transactions, then fine. But there aren't many businesses now which are sustainable due to quick wins. You may not see that person again, but you're most likely not going to receive a referral from them in the event that they live to regret a decision they felt pushed into. Because if they aren't given time, and they feel as if they have been press-ganged into it, then they will hold you responsible – and therein lies the problem.

## GIVE PEOPLE TIME TO FAIL

People need to know that they can fail. They need to know that they can make decisions and that they will be supported. It means offering suggestions, trying new approaches and not being afraid of the unknown, untried or untested.

This doesn't mean being foolhardy or reckless. It does mean applying the other principles here – taking the time to think, time to make decisions and taking responsibility. But it also means accepting that we won't always be successful and that sometimes failing is needed.

In fact, I'll go one step further than that to say that failing is necessary for longer-term success. It's essential in the development of a person or an idea. Here are a few examples of high profile 'failures' just in case you needed the reassurance that even the most successful people don't always get it right :

### J.K. ROWLING
12 publishers rejected the manuscript of *Harry Potter*.

She went on to sell more than 400 million copies of the Harry Potter books worldwide.

### OPRAH WINFREY
She was fired from her television reporting job as she was deemed not suitable for television.

And went on to become one of the most recognised names in television.

### MICHAEL JORDAN
He was cut from his high school basketball team.

And went on to become one of the greatest basketball players of all time.

### ALBERT EINSTEIN
His teachers called him 'slow', he didn't speak until he turned four and didn't read until he was seven.

He went on to develop the general theory of relativity, one of the two pillars of modern physics.

### CLINT EASTWOOD

In 1954 he was fired from Universal Studios when a couple of studio executives noticed his Adam's apple was too big.

He went on to become one of the most famous actors of the last 50 years.

### STEVEN SPIELBERG

He was rejected by the University of Southern California, three times.

He went on win Academy Awards for *Schindler's List* and *Saving Private Ryan.*

### STEPHEN KING

His first book, *Carrie*, was rejected 30 times.

He went on to sell more than 350 million books worldwide.

Too much success is not healthy and, in failing, we learn: we learn what works, what doesn't, what our strengths and weaknesses are; ultimately failing allows us to grow. But it's a mindset change, a paradigm shift. All too often, failure is seen as negative and this is reinforced time and time again. Instead, we should see failure as a step on the journey towards success. If you want to provide real value and significance to your customers, encourage them to try new things, ensure they see failure as a necessary step on the path to success, and show them by demonstrating this approach.

# GIVE PEOPLE TIME TO SUCCEED

Which brings us nicely to the next element of 'time': some things just take time to become successful.

Successful sales people, successful customers, successful relationships, successful businesses: instant success stories are not the norm and often they disappear as quickly as they arrived. Businesses, initiatives, groups and individuals rarely become successful overnight.

This can be difficult to accept, especially when we want results and success yesterday. It's hard for results-orientated people in general, but especially hard for managers and executives who just want more... and quickly. But it's true. Sometimes we just need time. Give people time to fail and time to succeed. Assuming you build your relationships and select your customers, people and opportunities based on a sound set of criteria, then the investment will pay off in the long run.

## The Case of the Yellow Dog

Alison Hardingham is Director of Business Psychology at Yellow Dog Consulting. In addition to running her own successful consulting firm, Alison works as visiting Professor at Henley Business School. Alison has published eight books in her field and her most recent book, *The Coach's Coach*, has become a standard text for many leadership and coaching development qualifications. She specialises in Executive Coaching.

What makes Alison so special is that she can take a group of individuals – strangers – and, within minutes, put them at ease and bring a sense of calm to the group. She can encourage them to be open, to share and to exchange views and ideas with incredible finesse and, having been one of those students, I believe she's able to do so by understanding and applying Genuine Curiosity.

She's not just interested in people, she's curious to learn – what they think and what they have to say. When she talks to you, you know that it's not about her but about you. What's more, she means it. It's genuine. She doesn't judge anyone; she just asks great questions and listens. And by giving people time she provides an environment in which you can feel like the most important person in the world – the only person in the world. She cares about other people and it's this combination which is so powerful.

Critically, Alison applies the same principles whether she meets you for the first time, teaches you on one of her programmes, coaches or talks to you as a prospective client. She is one of the UK's leading Executive Coaches with a client base which spans multi-billion dollar, worldwide companies.

## SELLING IS THE TRANSFER OF TRUST

Selling is the transfer of trust and so, by adopting these approaches, you begin to build the trust that can become a platform for success. The essence of this approach is founded on the principles of coaching for performance and, at the heart of it, relationships built on trust.

The importance of developing and using fundamental communication skills cannot be over-estimated, yet they are often discarded in favour of a quicker, more direct approach, based on the need to achieve and the pressures of day-to-day life.

But there is no short-cut to building customer loyalty and relationships; you have to be willing to invest, to put the time in and use methods that take an interest in the other person's world, with the aim of adding value and contributing to their success. After all, it is mutual success that ultimately leads to better, longer-term relationships.

## START TO BECOME SIGNIFICANT

Getting Genuinely Curious is at the heart of the *GO NAKED* approach and is an underlying theme throughout. Having the desire to put the other person at the centre of your thinking is key. If you work on anything, work on this.

Authentic people build authentic relationships. If you've got the confidence to focus on the other person; if you're brave enough to learn about the other person and so allow them to learn about you in return; and if you're comfortable with giving people time, you have the opportunity to build great relationships in a way which adds value and significance to others – and there is no greater calling than to add value and significance to others.

But as with everything here, it requires you to take a risk: to challenge conventional wisdom; to try new approaches and be willing to fail; to be brave and go places you haven't been before. So commit to action today in all of your relationships. If you give more than you're required to give to your relationships, you will receive more than you need in return.

# KEY MESSAGES

In order to Get Genuinely Curious:

- Care more about the other person than you do yourself
- Be authentic
  - Know your values
  - Tell your story
  - Communicate your position
- Give people time
  - Time to listen
  - Time to answer questions
  - Time to think
  - Time to make decisions
  - Time to fail
  - Time to succeed

# OFFER SOMETHING DIFFERENT

*What counts in life is not the mere fact that we have lived.*
*It is what difference we have made to the lives of others*
*that will determine the significance of the life we lead.*
NELSON MANDELA, FORMER PRESIDENT OF SOUTH AFRICA

People don't want boring anymore. They don't just want to hear 'yes'. They want to hear something new, something different. They want to have their thinking challenged.

That's new for many of us – for those of us who've grown up believing the mantra that 'the customer is always right' or those of us who feel uncomfortable in providing an alternative opinion at the risk of upsetting the other person.

That's exactly what needs to happen now. In the new age we're now living and working in, boring, safe and middle of the road just won't cut it anymore.

# THE PROBLEM WITH THE MIDDLE OF THE ROAD

*The Karate Kid* was a cult move in the 1980s. For those of you not familiar with the plot, it charts the story of Daniel, an American teenager who moves to a new neighbourhood and attracts the attention of the local school bullies. Having an interest in Karate, he enlists the help of the apartment complex's janitor, Mr Miyagi, who is not only a handyman but a Karate master. In addition to helping him overcome his aggressors, Mr Miyagi also teaches him about life through a series of valuable lessons.

In one such scene below, Daniel (san) is about to begin practice. Mr Miyagi turns to him and asks:

Mr Miyagi:     Now, ready?

Daniel:          Yeah, I guess so.

Mr Miyagi:     [Sighs] Daniel-san, must talk. [They both kneel]

Mr Miyagi:     Walk on road.

Walk left side, safe. Walk right side, safe. Walk middle, sooner or later [makes squish gesture] get squish just like grape. Here, karate, same thing. Either you karate do 'yes' or karate do 'no'. You karate do 'guess so' [makes squish gesture], just like grape. Understand?

Daniel:          Yeah, I understand.

Mr Miyagi:     Now, ready?

Daniel:          Yeah, I'm ready

Almost 30 years after the film's release, this lesson applies now more than ever to relationships and business.

## GETTING AWAY FROM THE MIDDLE

There is no longer a place for middle of the road. Middle of the road is not safe anymore. Middle of the road leads to a terminal point, somewhere in the distance where the majority are. But if you want to get off the road, if you want to experience what life has to offer, and if you want to offer something different to people in your network, then middle of the road is not the place to be.

In building relationships and in looking for ways to work with others in the most productive way possible, we need to help get the best out of them. Very simply, if we get the best out of someone else then we create significance to them and with that the opportunities become boundless.

The problem for many, though, is in knowing how to do that.

*How do you as a sales person offer something different in what is most likely a crowded market place?*

*How can you begin to create value and significance in someone else's world when you're selling a similar product or service as the next ten people in line?*

The whole premise of GO NAKED is based on the understanding that by stripping away limiting beliefs and conventional wisdom we can develop stronger, more successful relationships. This is what is required to offer something different. We are not defined by the product we sell but the value we create. We can learn a lot from two basic principles of coaching: the need to raise *awareness;* and ensure that the other person is the one taking *responsibility* for their decisions. We do this by challenging them – challenging their assumptions and their limiting beliefs – to provide a different perspective and different set of options than they would otherwise have seen. In addition, we support them to create a positive environment for growth and one in which they can take responsibility.

## ADOPT A COACHING APPROACH

Coaching is based on developing two elements – awareness and responsibility – which is what makes working with a coach so beneficial. But imagine if you could also play that role with your customers or others you were working and communicating with? How valuable would that be? To be able to put the other person central to the discussion so that you were able to help raise their awareness to new and different options but also allow them to take responsibility for the choices and the decisions they make.

Now people talk about 'adding value' and we'll discuss this concept of value in more detail in a later chapter, but for the moment let's just say this: if you were able to change the nature of your relationship with another – whether that be a customer or anyone else for that matter – so that you could raise their awareness to different options through asking great questions, then for them to take responsibility, what a great relationship that would be. Forget the transaction, forget the features and benefits – you've just added more value to your customer than they ever thought possible, and in doing so you've taken steps to further develop the trust which must exist between you both for a fruitful relationship.

And that's ultimately what selling is – the transfer of trust.

## RAISE AWARENESS – ASK GREAT QUESTIONS

We talked previously about how genuine interest comes from a desire to understand better the person and their circumstances. Raising awareness comes from the same place: a desire to understand better the person and their circumstances. It comes from listening actively to the person in front of you and responding to the words they use and the manner in which they use them. It begins and ends with questions – the quality of which are paramount.

What are great questions?

They differ depending on the person, but in general great questions raise the other person's awareness of a view or options they previously weren't aware of.

Here are some examples of the types of questions that can be used to raise awareness.

### Motivate and stimulate

These are the types of questions which provoke a reaction or an opinion. They should be relevant to the person you're with and linked to their area of interest or specialty. They could be based on the latest relevant news or trends and, of course, asked with Genuine Curiosity.

*The greatest opportunity within your industry today
is reported to be X. What are your views on that?*

*This segment of the market is well documented to be
growing exponentially. How do you assess your chances
of being able to capitalise on that in the long-term?*

*What is your vision for you/your business in five years' time?*

## Risks and consequences

When you ask about risks and consequences, you are potentially highlighting the impact of not acting or changing to capitalise on an opportunity. They should be asked from a neutral position and one based in your desire to help raise their awareness to other possibilities.

*What are the risks of not taking any action?*

*What do you see as the possible negative impact
of not taking advantage of this opportunity?*

*To what extent would your ability to develop
be hindered if you didn't act now?*

## Benefits and rewards

The reverse of the risk and consequences types of questions, the benefits and rewards questions provide focus around what the positive consequences or upside could be from following a particular course of action. Again, this isn't necessarily about you sharing your view at this point, or trying to elicit a particular response from a biased position, but simply about taking a position which challenges thinking.

*What benefits do you see in taking this action?*

*How would your circumstances improve if
you took advantage of this opportunity?*

*To what extent would you be able to achieve your
goals if you follow this path?*

## Remove pre-held or limiting beliefs

Perhaps one of the most powerful ways to ask questions of others is so as to disarm them of limiting beliefs. Often the only reason people don't follow a course of action is the barriers they themselves put up; because of perceived issues rather than genuine problems. Not only do these barriers stop them from taking action, but they restrict their ability to think more broadly in the first place. Crack this one and you can make a huge difference.

*If you knew you couldn't fail, what ideas would
you have as to how to approach this?*

*If you knew there was no risk involved, how would
that change the way you think about this?*

*If you could guarantee success, what options would you consider?*

## YOU HOLD THE KEY

There is no real shortcut here. It is down to asking questions that accomplish the above, listening to the answers and reacting. Questioning is a skill which, like anything else, requires practice. You can't expect to develop it without giving it some focus, attention and regular practice.

It is such a fundamental skill that we take it for granted. We assume that it's almost too basic to warrant further development, but it really does hold the key. And the great thing with this skill is that it can be practised anywhere, at any time with anyone. At work, at home; with friends, family, colleagues, customers, bosses. And the more you practise with these different ideas, the more you will see how powerful a tool they really are in raising awareness. Once you do that, you hold the key to success and, more importantly, you also give the other person the key too.

## USING THE FOUR LENSES

There are times when we could all improve our responses to certain situations. By using four alternative lenses it is possible to pre-empt that retrospective disappointment by looking at alternative options prior to making a decision. Used correctly, these lenses can provide a different perspective other than your original view and offer another way to raise awareness.

1. **THE REVERSE LENS** – imagine looking at the situation or options from the other person's perspective.

*How would the other person involved in the situation view this?*

This is an extremely useful approach if you are having any type of disagreement or conflict with someone else. Take the time to see the situation from their perspective. What are they seeing that you aren't? What can they see which is influencing the way they think?

**2. THE TELESCOPIC LENS** – this helps you take a longer-term view of the situation.

*How would you view this situation in 12 months' time?*

This can be particularly helpful in the event that things haven't gone well, for whatever reason. Taking a long-term view can help put things into context. This type of approach can be great during idea generation or planning sessions. What will things look like in 12 months and how could you capitalise on them?

**3. THE WIDE LENS** – this helps broaden out your thinking.

*What options haven't you considered yet?*

This sort of questioning helps when you're feeling at a dead-end, when you're out of ideas, when you don't know what to try next. Don't limit your thinking; instead, use this type of question to free yourself or others.

**4. THE THIRD-EYE LENS** – this provides objectivity, from someone removed from the situation.

*How would someone else viewing the situation assess it?*

You can use this lens and questions with anyone, including yourself, and they can provide some much needed objectivity on the situation.

*How would a fresh pair of eyes see this – what would they see that we're missing? What ideas would they have that we don't?*

The four lenses are a tool, but here again we see that the key to this is asking great questions – questions that provide a different perspective and questions that remove barriers. Forget open and closed questions. Instead, focus on asking great questions. By getting people to change their perspective on the situation you provide a different set of options.

## AT THE RISK OF ROCKING THE BOAT

I'm sure you've seen it a thousand times before. Someone tells you their plans, perhaps with a degree of conviction, and you think, 'Hmmm… I know that's not the most proven way,' or 'Well that could be an option, but what about x, y or z?' But at the same time you're considering these thoughts another voice appears and says, 'Don't be stupid! If you challenge them now you'll really rock the boat! Just let them keep going.'

Sound familiar?

The problem with this approach is that it's fine in the short-term, but a disaster waiting to happen in the longer-term. So often the relationships we are building are exactly that – being built – and so should be done in a way that stands the test of time. That means that people will want to continue to work with us as time goes by, as others come and go and new products or services appear onto the scene.

To do this we have to be prepared to create significance and one way to do so is to challenge people's thinking.

Now let's be clear here, this isn't about being rude, disrespectful, discourteous or anything similar. It's just that, at times, everyone including customers and potential customers need to know there are options – other options. They need to have their thinking challenged too, just like anyone else. Why allow someone to wander down a less attractive, less viable path when you know there may be another route?

## IT'S A DEAD CERT!

Let's reverse the situation for a moment. You're talking to someone about how you've stumbled across a great way to build your business and that is to set up a social media presence, specifically through Facebook. 'It a dead cert!' you say enthusiastically, 'Everyone's doing it... and what's even better is, it's free advertising... the more friends and likes you have the more potential customers... easy!'

What issues do you see in this flawless plan? Here are just a few:

- Any social media activity needs to be part of an integrated marketing approach
- Social media alone will not drive leads or conversion rate
- Content needs to be relevant and updated frequently
- There should be a dedicated person responsible for managing content
- With the plethora of social media networks, one is unlikely to be sufficient and therefore there should be a broader approach

But if this person is a supplier of yours, or a friend in business, and they don't challenge your thinking, what then? Well, most likely you set off down this path and fail. Even if you've just wasted time, time is money. But imagine they had raised your awareness to the different options, given you their insight and shared their ideas. You're under no obligation to adhere to them, but at least you have a different perspective on the situation. Often, we can all move along with our heads down, unaware of the alternative options around us, in the middle of the road.

## NOW THE 'BUT'

It can't all be challenge. There has to be an element of support in there and, I would say, with equal measure. When there is too much challenge you can actually stunt development. Conversely, too much support and you don't encourage the thinking that will lead to greater development.

So the key is to get the balance right between challenge and support, because with that balance comes the opportunity for growth. And so a great way for us to provide value and opportunity for growth to customers is by offering challenge: challenging assumptions, limiting beliefs and options for their development, and then supporting their decision making.

Challenge in this context should really be seen as a 'freeing' activity – a way to open the mind and explore more options; to remove limiting beliefs or negative assumptions which are held, which restrict the growth of the other person. And be under no illusion, this is a skill which needs to be developed over time.

# GIVE RESPONSIBILITY – LET THEM MAKE THE DECISIONS

## *Re-spon-si-bil-i-ty*
*The state or fact of being responsible,*
*answerable, or accountable for something*
*within one's power, control, or management.*

WWW.DICTIONARY.COM

I want to differentiate here between passing off responsibility – your responsibility – and allowing other people the opportunity to take responsibility for the decisions they make. It's the latter I am advocating.

Because in giving the other person responsibility you put them in control. They become the masters of their own destiny. They make a decision or series of decisions and then take responsibility for the delivery.

Why is this important? All too often people are willing to, or encouraged to, trade – trade their responsibility for someone else's knowledge or information or a decision. But giving away responsibility is seldom, if ever, a worthwhile approach. For example, someone may say, 'Tell me what I should do', 'What would *you* do in my position?' or 'What do *you* think is the best option?' What they're actually saying is, 'Please can you make the decision, tell me what to do and keep the responsibility for its outcome!' What they're also saying is, 'If it doesn't work out, it was never my idea in the first place!'

The best way to allow someone to take responsibility is to let them decide. So what does that mean within a selling relationship?

It means letting the other person make the choice or decision and then supporting that choice. It does not mean forcing an agenda or decision; it does not mean making the choice for them; and it does not mean 'closing' with a series of *your* actions or next steps. It must be an agreed set of actions that allows both parties to take ownership and responsibility for the individual elements.

Of course this doesn't mean you can't take responsibility for yourself. You absolutely should and it's a trait clearly seen in successful people. But you shouldn't take responsibility for other people's decisions and actions. That's their job. Don't interfere.

## A TRUE STORY

Two people are discussing a business challenge – in this instance they are manager and employee. They go back and forth as to the best course of action and, whilst they are both working towards the same outcome, their methods for how to get there vary. They are both committed to their individual methods and in the end the manager says, 'Just do it my way.'

In that split second, what happens?

The manager has traded his employee's responsibility for his preferred course of action. You now have someone tasked with carrying out the activity who is not bought in to it and not feeling wholly responsible. If it goes well, so what? It was their manager's idea anyway and he'll take the credit. If it fails, big deal… it wasn't the employee's idea in the first place and he didn't even want to do it!

Let's look at a second scenario.

A customer and sales person are discussing a new product and whether or not the customer should adopt it versus that which they currently use. It's an 'upsell' for the sales person, the customer is already using a less expensive version. The sales person has a target on this new product and so is keen for the customer to use it. The customer has been pleased with the results of the current product and really sees little value in changing at the moment. The customer turns to the sales person and says, 'We're tight on budget at the moment so we don't need the added expense, plus I'm happy with what I've got today. What do you think I should do?'

What do you say?

What are the consequences, both now and potentially later?

Take a moment to think it through.

It's not that there's a right or wrong answer here; as with most things, it's all about style and what you're comfortable with. Maybe you answer, or maybe you ask another question to raise their awareness to different options and remove limiting beliefs. As with the first example, if you tell the customer what to do you are trading his responsibility for your advice, which means that he is foregoing ownership of the decision. I'm of the opinion that being driven by short-term targets and allowing them to impact on your decision-making and judgment, especially when it comes to this subject, is not a sustainable approach.

Ultimately, you will end up being left on the shelf, as an example of a time gone by, as much as your products will. Conversely, if you focus on understanding, on asking great questions and on removing limiting beliefs you can provide an alternative perspective that ultimately will result in the customer taking responsibility for their decisions and supporting the development of your future relationship and business.

## BALANCE THE NEED FOR CHALLENGE AND SUPPORT

If we want people to grow we have to challenge and support. Challenge their thinking and support their decision-making. Allow them room to fail if necessary.

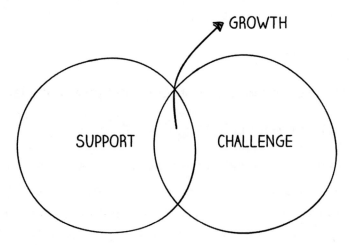

Sometimes the balance is too one-sided: too much challenge and not enough support; or too much support and not enough challenge.

If we don't support enough, we restrict thinking, we demoralise people and we risk stunting their development. No one wants to hear challenge after challenge after challenge – it's boring, monotonous and it's a sure fire way to negatively impact a relationship. So it has to be balanced with the right level of support in order to constructively create freedom of thinking.

If, on the other hand, you don't challenge enough, where is the value? How are you stimulating growth or different thinking? How are you contributing to the discussion? If you just go on saying 'yes' and supporting people, you risk becoming passive, loosing significance and doing so quickly – especially if you're in business-to-business sales where it's no longer just about the core product or service you are selling. It's about so much more than that. Customers and businesses want more, they are demanding more, they expect more and they want to be challenged. They want to know how others are doing it, know what latest trends you have seen and know if there is a better way. They want to see you on one side of the road.

But this is the same for any relationship – any strong, positive relationship.

In order to encourage growth we challenge to liberate thinking, remove limiting beliefs and dismiss conventional wisdom. Then we support the choices made and provide a safe environment in which to do so.

In following this approach, we can and will encourage growth.

## Engineering, Marketing and Selling

Raphael Pascaud is Vice President at a multi-national medical device company. He started his career as an engineer after graduating with a PhD from Cardiff University. After spending his initial years working as part of a Research and Development team he moved into sales and marketing roles, taking on more senior roles before being appointed to director level and above.

It is perhaps this combination of engineering – with its structured, methodical and analytical approach – combined with the creativity and strategic thinking developed in marketing, augmented by the commercial acumen gained through his sales roles that make him the leader he is today.

Because there's no doubt about it, he could run any domestic or multi-national company out there.

One of Raphael's core strengths and one of the reasons he has been so successful is his ability to challenge and support, to raise awareness to different options and to give others responsibility for the decision-making.

He does this with his team and his broader organisation and he does this with his customers. He can stand in front of a roomful of customers and challenge their thinking; he can take any one of those people one-on-one and support their decision-making – giving them the chance to try something new or adopt a different approach.

Perhaps it's the engineer in him that allows him to analyse, focus on a point and then challenge using a combination of the types of questions reviewed earlier. It may be the marketer in him which allows him to constantly take a different lens to a situation and change the perspective of the others in the room. And it may be the great salesman in him which means that he's not afraid to take a risk, to ask a difficult question or highlight an alternative.

But importantly he accepts that it won't always work out, that there will be mistakes along the way; that in order for people to be successful they will sometimes fail. But he's ok with that, in fact he encourages it amongst his team and his customers.

Next time you're with someone and your goal is to understand, approach your questions as an engineer – by being methodical and analytical; as a marketer – by being creative and using different lenses; and as a sales person – by being commercially focused and willing to take a risk.

## TOUGH TIMES

Times are tough and the news is littered with stories about the current economic conditions. It's commonplace, regardless of where we go, and something we see pretty much every day in one way or another. Whether the story be about austerity, increasing unemployment or inflation, decreasing output, interest rates or deficit reduction plans, it's something we've all been affected by, whether personally or professionally.

So how are these things affecting relationships, business and sales?

We're seeing a reduction in prices to customers; we're seeing the attempt in some quarters to force commoditisation; we're seeing standardisation of product and rationalisation of supplier base.

Businesses are trying to react and combat these conditions – from cutting spending, to cutting personnel numbers, to restructuring organisations; creating new positions, outsourcing departments or amalgamating business units.

But let's not forget that we are in the business of people and that selling is a contact sport, so ultimately it will be the people who make the difference.

Because of this, we must find a way to offer something different. We must keep searching for ways to add value and significance to others which extends beyond being defined by our company or product. To *GO NAKED* is to create significance and value to others and this core principle is based on adopting a coaching approach to the way in which we interact and sell. It is based on awareness, responsibility, challenge and support. Coupled with Genuine Curiosity, this arms you with the opportunity to step out from the majority and Offer Something Different.

## KEY MESSAGES

In order to Offer Something Different:

- Adopt a coaching approach
- Challenge to raise awareness by asking questions which:
  - Motivate and stimulate
  - Explore risks and consequences
  - Highlight benefits and rewards
  - Remove pre-held or limiting beliefs
- Offer a different perspective by using the four lenses:
  - The Reverse lens
  - The Telescopic lens
  - The Wide lens
  - Third Eye lens
- Support and allow others to take responsibility for their decisions

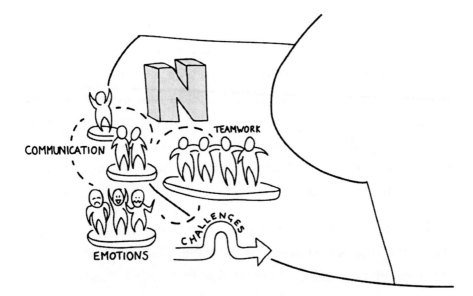

# NOTICE AND MANAGE YOURSELF AND OTHERS

*If your emotional abilities aren't in hand, if you don't have self-awareness, if you are not able to manage your distressing emotions, if you can't have empathy and have effective relationships, then no matter how smart you are, you are not going to get very far.*
DANIEL GOLEMAN, AUTHOR, PSYCHOLOGIST, AND SCIENCE JOURNALIST

## THERE ARE A LOT OF INTELLIGENT PEOPLE OUT THERE

There are more university graduates than ever before. Official UK Government data showed that 558,898 people applied to universities in 2013, 3.5 percent up from the year before. In

2010, 334,890 people graduated from UK universities, rising from 319,260 in 2008, and many of these graduates went on to study for a second or Master's degree. In fact, it's become increasingly common to go straight from a first degree to a second degree as a way to try and get ahead in the employment market. Regardless of your opinion of university courses or their graduates, you can't argue with the fact that there are now more academically qualified people out there than ever before.

Having bright people around you is great. But intellect only gets you so far. It gets you a seat at the table. The thing that is more important than intellect when it comes to the development of relationships is emotional intelligence – in other words, the ability to identify, use, understand, and manage emotions in positive ways to relieve stress, communicate effectively, empathise with others, overcome challenges, and defuse conflict. Ironically, none of this is taught in schools, universities or many organisations.

## WHY 'NOTICING' IS KEY

Neurolinguistic programming (NLP) brings together a number of different disciplines with the goal of exploring and explaining how people really work. In understanding more, the aim is to help people use that knowledge to improve their self-management. A key determinant of this is emotional intelligence, which impacts many different aspects of your daily life such as the way you behave and the way you interact with others.

I'm going to use the word 'notice' a lot, as I believe that this is the first step on the road to a higher degree of self-management; that it starts with being able to notice yourself and others. With that in mind, I want to look at two distinct areas: firstly, how we can improve the way we notice ourselves and each other; secondly, what can we do to improve the way we manage ourselves to increase our chances of success, and the way we manage our relationships to add greater significance.

The reality is that if you can better notice and manage yourself and others – if you can achieve a higher level of emotional intelligence – your chances of creating significant, successful selling relationships multiply exponentially.

## Accident and Emergency

My first sales job was selling disposable medical products into UK hospitals and my sales territory was South London, Kent and Sussex. One of the products we sold was a disposable laryngoscope. A laryngoscope is used when people are being put under a general anaesthetic. It looks a bit like a hammer with a flattened hook on the top, and is used by the anaesthetist to gently move the tongue to one side so that they can view the back of the throat and place a tube down the airway when the patient requires breathing support. In addition to having them in Theatre and in Critical Care Units, they are also held on Accident and Emergency departments.

It was my first sales call of the day and my boss was out with me, so I was ready to impress. I hadn't booked an appointment with anyone in Accident and Emergency, but that was ok for me, I wasn't going to be perturbed.

I wandered into the department with all the certainty in the world and headed for who I assumed to be the Consultant. As I approached him, I reached out my hand to introduce myself to him. He turned around and I caught a glimpse of his name badge: I had struck gold. Not only was he the lead clinician on the department but his first name was also Michael. I couldn't fail!

(At this point let me pause and remind you that a medical Consultant will have, on average, trained for nine years after completing their medical degree – so around 13 years in total. Once they qualify as a Consultant they once again become a 'Mr' as a sign of seniority to those with 'Dr' in their title.)

I reached out my hand to introduce myself to him by saying, 'Hi Mike!'

My boss looked stunned.

'Mike' was stunned.

But I kept going, like a madman, straight into my sales call. 'Ok, I'm here today to tell you about how our laryngoscope will change your life!'

There are a number of points during this account of my visit to Accident and Emergency that will make your toes curl, from the fact that I walked uninvited into a hospital department without any regard for the staff or patients; to the fact that I introduced myself to a senior clinician as if I'd just met him on a night out in the local pub; to the fact that despite these faux pas I just kept going and pushing my agenda. If your toes curled, that's good. You've got more emotional intelligence than I did that day, which, by the way, wasn't the most successful in my sales career.

## YOU NEED TO WORK OUT

Emotional intelligence affects all aspects of our lives, business and personal, and both areas require focus and development. Even the most skilled people in this area must continue to work at it. It's like a muscle that you can strengthen, but which you must continue to exercise.

While there are exceptions and outliers, the most intelligent people are not necessarily the most successful or fulfilled. We can all think of examples of people who are stunningly bright, but when it comes to interacting with others socially you can almost guarantee that they will say the wrong thing at the wrong time. Perhaps they're known for it and it's a bit of a running joke, but the reality is that these individuals will never reach the potential they could, had they taken some time to develop this skill set.

This ability is especially relevant to people who work in a professional selling capacity as their success will be determined by their ability to do these things effectively.

## FOUR PARTS

Emotional intelligence can be broken down into four parts. The first is self-awareness, but as you can see from the diagram, being self-aware (noticing yourself) impacts your social awareness (how you notice others) and your self-management (how you control and manage yourself), which all lead to how well you can manage your relationships and get the best out of them.

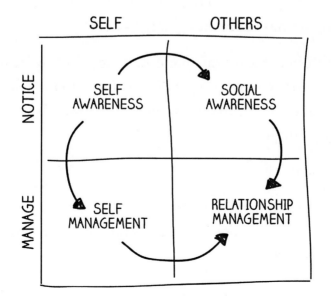

# 1. Self-awareness

Self-awareness is concerned with accurate-self assessment. In other words, being able to notice and understand the way you feel, to recognise your own limiting beliefs – the thoughts and feelings that hold us back and constrain us – and have the confidence to believe in yourself and create freedom from those limiting beliefs.

Ask yourself, to what extent are you able to notice your own emotions and how they affect your  mindset and behaviour? How aware are you of your strengths and weaknesses – are you capable of identifying them and being ok with them? How confident are you? What's stopping you? Are you able to break through your limiting beliefs?

## THE ROAD NOT TAKEN

How many times have you gone to do something, paused and then decided against if? How many times have you gone to send something, start something, publish something, submit something or make something only to decide 'no'?

And how often have you made that decision for fear that it won't be liked? Out of concern that it's not good enough? Due to worry that you may look foolish? Or through anxiety that others may laugh?

I know I have.

These feelings and these aversions are, in part, a result of the way we've been schooled, taught and indoctrinated through our working lives.

Do any of these examples sound familiar:

*Don't get too big for your boots.*
*Don't put your head above the parapet.*
*Don't try to be too clever.*
*Don't try to be better than you are.*
*Don't take risks.*

Or how about these:

*Do wait your turn.*
*Do worry what others think.*
*Do wait to be asked.*
*Do blend into the crowd*

If any of the above prevents you from sending, starting, publishing, submitting, or making, then you're culpable of giving into this conventional wisdom at one time or another.

The point is that doing something new, trying something new is scary. Of course it is and that's the way of it. But once you start, once you get going and once you generate momentum, those feelings subside, your comfort zone increases and you move on to do more of whatever it was you wanted to do in the first place.

Because that's the thing. If we try more, do more, our tolerance for the scary increases. We're less impacted and less likely to be knocked off our course. Try less, do less and our tolerance for the scary decreases. We're more likely to say no – that we're not good enough, clever enough or strong enough.

How many new and innovative approaches could you have shared? How many better ways to do things could you have demonstrated? How much could you have connected to or resonated with an audience?

If the road not taken is done so because there is visible danger ahead, so be it. But if it's through fear of what *might* lie ahead then our outlook will constantly be constrained and possibilities limited.

In business and sales, having the self-awareness to break through these limiting beliefs is critical in unlocking the potential power which lies dormant in so many of us.

## 2. Self-management

Self-management focuses on the degree of self-control you have. Can you handle yourself in difficult or pressured situations? How capable are you of managing how you feel, your behaviours and emotions? How much willpower do you have – can you resist temptation? How likely are you to follow through on commitments?

In addition, it's related to our adaptability – the degree to which we can adjust to different circumstances; how much drive and desire to achieve we have; and the extent to which we can demonstrate initiative.

Imagine the scene…

You're sitting on the motorway, in the middle lane. You've overtaken a couple of cars on the inside lane and you're just about to drift back across to take your position on the inside.

At that moment, you feel a pressure on your car, as someone speeds inside of you, bisects you and the car in front, and speeds into the outside lane.

In that spit second, how do you react?

Do you have a strong feeling? Do you explode in anger? Do you feel upset? Can you sense frustration inside yourself?

Now the important question. What does your reaction tell you about *you*?

## HOW YOU RESPOND IS A CHOICE

In fact, it's the only choice you have, and it can be represented as:

$$Stimulus + Response = Consequences$$

For any given stimulus – something that happens to you – the only thing you can control is your response and therefore *that* should be your focus. More often than not, you have no control over the stimulus – the action which occurs. The only thing you can control is your response, and any consequences are a direct result of your chosen response.

Note the key words here – *your chosen response*. For you do have a choice and how you choose to respond tells you a lot about *you* and your mindset.

You can't control someone cutting you up on the motorway, or your boss asking for a piece of work immediately, or a customer rejecting you. You can't control someone else's behaviour. However, you can control how you react to that action or stimulus.

Being able to notice those feelings, then consider and manage your reaction appropriately can set you apart from the majority.

If you can't notice and control your emotions, you'll be open to sudden changes in mood and temperament that can impact your ability to build relationships. One of the key drivers of this is stress, though it's a misconception that all stress is negative: there are two distinct types.

First, *Eustress*. This can be fun and exciting, especially in the short-term, like when skiing or mountain biking or rushing to meet a first date! Just the right amount of stress is stimulating and healthy and helps us perform tasks faster and better.

Second, *Distress*. This is the negative stuff and is to do with our reaction to stimuli, such as someone cutting you up on the motorway, or your boss asking for a piece or work to be done right away. It can come and go or hang around for longer.

It's the distress that we have to learn to manage better – to control our response to any given stimulus as a way to improve the chances of a successful outcome or consequences.

## LEARN TO NOTICE AND RESPOND TO YOUR FEELINGS

This is a great approach to dealing with a given stimulus because, while it allows you to notice certain feelings in yourself, it can be done whilst focusing on people around you. You can do this in a meeting, with a group of people, at a dinner party, at home – anywhere.

### Notice certain feelings

Just notice a given stimulus. It could be what someone else says, or how they say it. It could be the language they use or what they emphasise. It could be the way they sit, the way they look at you... it could be any number of things but the important things is just to notice it.

### Understand what your response to those feelings is

When you noticed it, how did you respond? What feelings did you get? Why did you notice it? For example, you may respond to someone being more assertive by sitting upright or your muscles tensing. You may respond to someone looking away by rolling your eyes. It can be anything – and nothing is right or wrong here. It's merely about having that self-awareness to notice something and then the self-management to control how you responded to that.

### Consider what those feelings mean for your development

The final piece is to think about what those feelings mean for your development. If you reacted to someone becoming more assertive in their tone by clenching your fists, what does that say about you and your development? If you roll your eyes at someone as they look away, what does that say about you and your development?

Again, no right or wrong answer here. No one will judge. It's about you, and you noticing how you respond to a given situation and taking the time to reflect on what that means for your development.

**Take the time to re-read this last section.**

This technique won't be easy to start with... it will require practice and reflection and it doesn't come naturally. But I assure you that the benefits of doing this for improving your self-awareness and self-management will be enormous in the long-run.

## 3. Social awareness

Social awareness is all about empathy. How aware are you of the emotions of other people? How capable are you of picking up on and reacting to non-verbal cues? How comfortable are you in a group or social setting?

This is the part that allows you to flourish within a group or organisation as you pick up on the cues of others around you. It can, in part, be determined by your propensity to want to serve others in terms of the value you create for them. If you want to create value for someone, developing this ability is key.

Being able to empathise or *notice others* is a real skill and the reason I'm emphasising the *noticing* element is that it is often the key. Let me give you some examples:

*Noticing that someone is uncomfortable in a particular situation*

*Noticing that the person in front of you is looking at their watch because they're late*

*Noticing when someone is providing non-verbal cues that they're happy to move on*

*Noticing when someone is upset*

*Noticing when someone is happy*

*Noticing when someone is looking for support*

*Noticing when someone is unsure and looking for alternative options*

*Noticing when someone is not giving you all the information*

## YOU NEED TO HAVE *THIN* SKIN

Most people have been given this advice at some point in their career. 'If you want to be successful in this business then you need thick skin.'

Put this phrase into any search engine and you'll discover that: if you're described as being thick-skinned it means that you're not easily offended and/or largely unaffected by the needs and feelings of other people; this is also linked to being insensitive.

I want to look at this advice and provide a different perspective on it.

If you take offence at someone or something, you're receiving a signal. It's a signal that something has taken place and you have had an emotional response to it. These signals are important indicators and our ability to be aware of them can be important. Equally important is your reaction to those signals.

Suggesting you should thicken your skin in this instance, as if to block out those feelings, is not great advice. Being able to manage these feelings is where the focus should be.

Equally, to suggest that you should do anything to ignore the needs or feelings of other people would be equally irresponsible for anyone dealing with people. The ability to sense the needs and feelings of others is inherent in those with a high degree of emotional intelligence.

Rather than thickening your skin as if to desensitise yourself, grow *thinner* skin. Be *more* sensitive to the needs and feelings of others and be *more* able to notice your own feelings, then manage them constructively.

## 4. Relationship management

This is critical to building strong, positive relationships, to be able to challenge constructively, to add significance to others and get the most out of people. How skilled are you at developing strong relationships? To what extent can you influence or inspire others? How comfortable are you at managing tension or conflict?

In the emotional intelligence quadrant above, everything drives towards improving relationships with others. It may be in the bottom right hand corner of the diagram, but it's the pinnacle of the system, built on the other foundational elements. Improving relationship management allows you to inspire and influence others; it allows you to lead and lead well; it gives you the opportunity to develop others; to manage change, to manage conflict; to build teams and collaborate.

### ENSURE THE GOAL IS TO UNDERSTAND

It's all too easy to assume you know what someone else is thinking or feeling. It can be based on preconceived ideas, the opinions of someone else or other information you have. By keeping your focus on the other person and actively listening, you improve the chances of developing a successful relationship.

Sometimes we're so busy trying to show how much we know that we forget the person in front of us or the people around us. Rather than focusing on showing how much you know, focus instead on trying to understand. If your mind drifts elsewhere, then notice it and quickly re-focus your attention on the other person.

Knowledge is the key to understanding. If the goal is to understand and that goal is met, then the rest will follow. Being able to actively listen is fundamental to this. There is listening and there is active listening. To do the latter, and to do it well, you should make a conscious effort to hear not only the words that another person is saying but to understand the complete message being sent, with a clear mind, free from clutter. You cannot allow yourself to become distracted by forming counter arguments that you'll make, or by becoming bored or distracted. Work to understand the complete message – the real message – before you respond.

Listening is one of those skills that, along with effective questioning, everyone knows they should do. However, because it is a fundamental principle – a simple principle – it is often not practised or taken for granted. Remember, it's one thing to know what to do at an intellectual level, and a completely different thing to actually take action and do so practically.

This requires practice and effort, so work on and be deliberate with your listening Remind yourself frequently that your goal is to really listen to and understand what the other person is saying with a clear mind. Remove any thoughts and behaviours that don't contribute to you really hearing what is being said, notice when your mind has wandered, and quickly re-focus. Clear your mind and give your full attention to the other person.

## The Warrior and the Master

A young and carefree warrior challenged a Zen master who was renowned for his skill as an archer. The young man was certainly capable and demonstrated remarkable proficiency when he hit the target's bull's eye on his first attempt. With equal finesse, he then raised his bow, fired, and split the first arrow with his second shot.

'There,' he said to the old man, 'see if you can beat that!'

The master did not draw his bow, but instead calmly motioned for the young warrior to follow him up the mountain. Curious about the old man's intentions, the warrior followed him high into the mountain until they reached a deep chasm, spanned by a rather flimsy and shaky log.

Calmly stepping out onto the middle of the unsteady bridge, the old master picked a far-away tree as a target. He raised his bow, and fired a clean, direct hit.

'Now it is your turn,' he said gracefully, as he stepped back onto the safe ground.

Staring with terror into the seemingly bottomless chasm, the young warrior could not force himself to step out onto the log, let alone shoot at the target.

'You have much skill with your bow,' the master said, sensing his challenger's predicament, 'but you have little skill with the mind that fires the shot.'

# DEVELOP YOUR MIND AS ONE OF YOUR SKILLS

While technical competence is a fundamental requirement of any job, emotional intelligence – noticing and managing yourself and others, and doing so well – can set you apart from the rest.

I've said that not embracing the need to develop emotional intelligence can negatively affect progression, personally and professionally. In addition, many companies are recruiting for emotional intelligence as well as the necessary qualifications and ability to perform the role. Performing in work is all about managing relationships and oneself – and this is the heart of emotional intelligence.

Research carried out by the Carnegie Institute of Technology shows that 85 percent of your financial success is due to skills in 'human engineering', your personality and ability to communicate, negotiate, and lead; only 15 percent is due to technical knowledge. Additionally, Nobel Prize-winning Israeli-American psychologist, Daniel Kahneman, found that people would rather do business with a person they like and trust than someone they don't, even if the likeable person is offering a lower quality product or service at a higher price.

To GO NAKED is to find ways in which to add significance to others. In order to add significance, you first have to notice and manage yourself before noticing and managing your relationship with others. Doing so gives you a head start over your competition. It allows you to get the best out of people and to offer them more, which will in turn resonate with them and lead to a virtuous circle of success.

# KEY MESSAGES

In order to Notice and Manage Yourself and Others:

- Understand that emotional intelligence trumps intellect
- Develop the four areas of emotional intelligence:
  - Notice yourself (self-awareness)
    - By breaking through limiting beliefs
  - Manage yourself (self-management)
    - By knowing that how you respond is within your control
  - Notice others (social awareness)
    - By having thin skin
  - Manage others (relationship management)
    - By ensuring the goal is to understand
- Work to develop your mindset as one of your skills

# AGREE GOALS

*Cherish your visions and your dreams*
*as they are the children of your soul, the*
*blueprints of your ultimate achievements.*
NAPOLEON HILL, AUTHOR

## TWO COMMON PROBLEMS

When it comes to our activity there are two common problems to overcome, whether that be in business life or in personal life.

### Issue number one

Often we don't share our goals, communicate them or agree them with the people who will be integral to their success. If the people around you are, or could be, important in the success of your goals, wouldn't it make sense to ensure they were involved in the discussion or design of them? In addition, this is a team sport – success relies on people. So in the spirit of what it means to *GO NAKED*, we have to be willing to reach out to other people, to share our hopes, dreams and ideas. In doing so, we offer ourselves the chance to be inspired further and the chance to inspire others with our goals.

## Issue number two

Too many people wake up every morning and just start working from where they left off yesterday, without stopping to think or consider the extent to which their activities are contributing towards their goals. They get in the car, head off, and just start working. They aren't working towards a longer-term vision, with goals and an associated plan.

They get caught up in just being busy. But of course, being busy doesn't necessarily mean adding greater value to their lives, business, colleagues, customers, friends or family. They get caught up in this cycle because of the belief that being busy equals valuable output; that by trying to do everything they may achieve something – and after all, that's better than nothing; and making the mistake of misinterpreting quantity of or time at work as being the only determining factor of successful output.

Many of us like to tell anyone who will listen just how busy we are, regardless of the measurement. Hours at the office, hours travelling, emails, phone calls, appointments. All the things we couldn't do: the time we weren't able to spend at home or doing the things we enjoy. Why do we do that? To make ourselves feel better? To alleviate pressure or stress? To share some of the burden or justify our behaviour? Perhaps all of the above. But being busy doesn't necessarily mean that there has been valuable output.

Being able to create a vision, set goals and an associated plan has long since been seen as a key determinant of a successful outcome. In this chapter, I want to tackle these two overarching problems. First, I want to dispel the myth that you shouldn't share your goals; and second, I want to provide a model for creating your vision, goals and plans – the *GO NAKED* way.

## WORKING ALONE

Imagine the scene...

You're crouched over your desk, a book protecting one side and your arm wrapped around your paper so no one can catch a glimpse of your work. On the other side of the classroom two people have adopted a different approach – they're edging their papers closer together so that they can both see each other's work. The teacher at the front of the class room sees them out of the corner of her eye and marches over. 'No conferring, no sharing!' she says angrily.

As you leave, someone turns to you and asks, 'How did it go?' You know how it went, but you aren't going to say – not truthfully or in its entirety, anyway. You don't want to say anything, just in case.

Fast forward a few years and things haven't changed. You've got an interview for university, an interview for a job, the chance to shine, the opportunity for a promotion, the chance for new business, the chance to win.

How do you approach this? Do you share the opportunity with others? Do you share how you plan to approach things? Do you open yourself out to others?

Or do you keep quiet, keep your arm around your work and never give a thought to sharing your ideas and plans, opportunities and challenges? You don't want to say anything, just in case. Just in case the teacher reprimands you.

As we look at how we've been conditioned, it's easy to see why we don't believe that the sum of the whole is greater than the parts. It's easy to see why we think that the best route to success is to conceal our plans for fear of someone copying them, or stealing them, or mocking them.

But there are two important things to consider here.

First, if you're worried about someone stealing your ideas, I've got news for you. The truth is that most people are too busy *not* working towards their own goals to worry about yours! Don't flatter yourself that your ideas are so much more wonderful and inspiring than theirs that other people are likely to change track and pursue your goal, rather than complete their own. In the event that yours is a brilliant idea, the chances are that you're already closer to its execution and much more passionate about it than anyone else could be.

Second, and more important, if you do have a working alone mindset, it's not an empowering one. If you can adopt an abundant mindset instead, the opportunities which present themselves will grow proportionally. If you have the courage to reach out to others, if you share your ideas and plans, if you ask for help and if you offer help in return, then 99 times out of a hundred, you will create more significance for yourself and others.

Hiding your ideas and work from others may have seemed like a good idea back in school; it might have been encouraged as you've grown, but it is unlikely to lead to success in your present or future. It won't be the fittest who prevail but those who have developed the most effective relationships and created the most value for others. It will be those who have an abundant mindset – those who understand that there is more than enough opportunity out there for all of us.

## ADJUSTED RECIPROCITY

If part of great goal setting is involving the right people, having the right people around you and sharing your goals with others, it would be great to do that with the people most likely to help you succeed, and who could share in your success.

It's a pretty simple message really – if you win, we win.

Goal setting, and great goal setting, is paramount to great sales people achieving success. In fact, you could broaden it further than just sales people – great goal setting is paramount to anyone achieving success.

Reciprocity is the way we respond to a positive action with another positive action. Reciprocity means that in response to friendly actions, people are frequently much nicer and much more cooperative. The reason I refer to 'adjusted reciprocity' is because, under the standard definition of reciprocity, there is almost an expectation that because you positively act, you will positively receive in return. My definition of 'adjusted reciprocity' suggests that you do so without expectation.

You just do.

You open up to people, you share with them and you add significance. By default, if you're open and willing to share your goals and ideas with people, many of them will be willing to help you to achieve them. Just don't expect it.

So what can we do to improve quality of output and add greater value and significance to ourselves, and the people around us? We can improve it by the way we set our goals, our personal and professional goals, and the manner in which we bring them to life. And by helping others do the same.

## KNOW YOUR OWN PERSONAL VISION AND GOALS

It may sound obvious, but you have to start with yourself. If you don't know what your vision is, how your goals support that vision and what your plans are to achieve those goals, you won't be able to help anyone else in the development or refinement of their vision and goals. Remember, this is all about how you can add value in the relationship – what better way to do this than to help others gain clarity of thinking in terms of what they want, the reasons why, and how they're going to get there.

## KNOW OR HELP DEFINE YOUR CUSTOMER'S VISION AND GOALS

The reality is that many of your customers and clients won't know what their vision and goals are, or they may know them in part, but not with full clarity. If you can follow the process for yourself, you can then help others to define their goals. In the event that they are already clear about their vision, your goal is to understand through Getting Genuinely Curious. The reason this is so important is that it gives you the chance to move on to the next section…

## AGREE YOUR JOINT VISION AND GOALS

If both of you can articulate your vision and goals, you can look for areas of synergy or commonality – areas where you can work together, help each other, so that you may both take steps towards the achievement of your goals. This is where the 'adjusted reciprocity' bit comes in. You can help each other.

All too often we behave as if we live in some sort of walled fortress, and we have a tendency to increase the size and substance of the walls. It's as if we've been conditioned from our school days to work individually: 'no looking at the work of the person next to you; don't help them – they need to do it themselves.'

But that is seldom the way to achieve success. We have to be willing to talk to others, share with others and look for mutually beneficial ways to help each other. We have to change our mindset to one of abundance – that there is more than enough out there for everyone and that by helping each other we can increase our chances of success.

# CREATING YOUR VISION – THE 'GO NAKED' WAY

## 1. Get Clear – Get clear on what you want and why you want it

*A leader has the vision and conviction*
*that a dream can be achieved. He inspires*
*the power and energy to get it done.*
**RALPH LAUREN, FASHION DESIGNER AND BUSINESS EXECUTIVE**

The first step is perhaps the most important, because gaining clarity at this point will act as your beacon as you move through the process. And note that there are two elements to this: there is the 'what' but there's also the 'why'.

Knowing what you want is essential, of course, and this should be what you want at the farthest point you can see. This point on the horizon should continue to guide you and therefore must be over the long-term. Just how long-term will depend on the size of the goal and your own personal situation. It provides clarity and focus and, importantly, it also defines what you are *not* going to do or *not* focus on.

Just as important as the 'what' is the 'why'. Why do you want to achieve your goal? For whilst the 'what' will guide your actions as your fixed point on the horizon, it is the 'why' which will motivate you to continue to work towards it. Anything in life worth having is likely to be a journey, with ups and downs along the way, and it's the 'why' that makes sure you keep going and working towards it.

If you say you want to earn £100,000 a year within five years, that's the 'what'. However, that 'what' is unlikely to keep you motivated during the tough times. They 'why' is different. Why do you want to earn £100,000? What will that allow you to do? Will it give you flexibility or choice? Will it allow you to go on more holidays or spend more time at home? This is where the 'why' becomes more important than the 'what'.

## THE STRATEGY OF 'WHY'

In January 2012 I decided I wanted to run a marathon.

I had never run that distance before, in fact the longest organised event I'd taken part in was 10 kilometres.

I picked an event, the Amsterdam Marathon, which was planned for 21st October 2012. I paid my money and entered. In addition, I knew I wanted to run it in under four hours, a typical target for amateur marathon runners.

For the proponents of SMART goal setting, I had everything I needed: I had a specific goal (running the Amsterdam Marathon on 21st October); it was measurable (I'd do it and plan to do it in under 4 hours); it was attainable at an acceptable cost (the entrance fee plus travel, accommodation and some new running gear); it was realistic (I'd done my 10K in around 43 minutes, so felt I could scale that performance over the greater distance); and it was time bound (I had to be ready for 21st October).

For anyone who's competed a marathon or any other endurance event, I'm sure you'll agree it's not SMART goal setting that gets you out of bed at 5am to do your training runs; it's not SMART goal setting that makes sure that you do the necessary distance and frequency of training runs; it's not SMART goal setting that keeps you going when your knees are sore and you can feel blisters developing in your instep; and its not SMART goal setting that makes you say 'no' to that beer or glass of wine while you're in the final stages of your training.

In these instances, SMART goals are pretty much useless.

But what does help you in all of these situations – what helps you in the achievement of anything – is a strong reason why.

I've always had a propensity to lack balance in my life and this gets worse when I'm busy at work. I could easily put in 18 to 19 hour days; get up at 5am and write emails; go to the office and work until 8 or 9pm; go home or back to my hotel and do some more emails until midnight. Sleep for five hours and then start again.

No exercise, no break, no relaxation, no balance.

When I decided to run the marathon, my 'why' was to get some balance in my life. I knew I couldn't just turn up and run without training, so signing up for that event forced me to get some balance. It forced me to decide and make a choice – to spend an hour, four days a week, going for a run. It's forced me to eat better, drink less and live a healthier day.

Having that 'why' kept me going when times were tough. Having that 'why' provided me with the extra motivation I needed. Without it, it would have been easy to stop, postpone or give up. My 'why' was so strong that it provided clarity in my thinking, planning and choices.

SMART goals are ideal if what you want is something specific, measurable, attainable, realistic and time-bound. They're great to create tactics. But they're not the whole answer. If you're after a strategy for success, you will need to follow a strategy of 'why'.

The next time you set your sights on a goal, give some thought to what your 'why' is.

Note: On 21st October 2012, I completed the Amsterdam Marathon in a time of three hours and 53 minutes, crossing the finish line in the Olympic Stadium, cheered on by my wife and son.

## 2. Open up – Open up to people who are important to you

> *It takes a lot of courage to show*
> *your dreams to someone else.*
> ERMA BOMBECK, AUTHOR

As I've said, there is a misperception that the way to achieve success is through creating a walled fortress of protection around yourself. But this is *GO NAKED*, which means putting yourself out there, taking a few risks, laying yourself bare and being willing to share your vision and goals with other people.

Some may tell you otherwise; they may say that you should keep your goals to yourself, perhaps because by sharing them you may create unnecessary additional pressure for yourself to achieve them. But you've read the chapter on the importance of being able to Notice and Manage Yourself and Others so you are already taking steps towards being able to manage pressure in a positive way.

Share your goals with people. Share them with people you care about and who care about you. Share them with people you are interested in and share them with people you think are interested in you. Share them with people whose opinion you value. Do so without expectation and thus with an open mind. You never know what may come of it: offers of help, support, advice, guidance, experience – take anything that comes your way and then decide which of them you want to leverage.

In addition, through sharing your goals with others you're holding yourself accountable. You can ask others to hold you accountable too. Either way, you're helping reinforce your commitment to succeed.

And just a note for those of you who worry someone might steal your goal…

Most people are too busy not achieving their own goals to worry about not achieving someone else's.

Think abundantly.

### 3. Never Doubt – Never doubt yourself and believe you can do it

*Believe you can and you're halfway there.*
THEODORE ROOSEVELT, 26TH PRESIDENT OF THE UNITED STATES

It's unlikely that everything will be plain sailing. It rarely is. And the chances are that there will be a few storms and squalls, a few failures along the way. But failing is only that if you don't learn from the experience, correct your course if need be, and keep full steam ahead. So this point is not so much of a 'how to' but a 'must do'. You must never doubt your ability to get the job done and to achieve your goal. If for any reason you do get a nagging doubt creeping into your mind, take steps to isolate the issue and deal with it.

Isolate the concern and then ask yourself a 'freeing question' by inserting the positive opposite:

*What steps could I take to make sure that I [insert positive opposite of the concern]?*

*If I knew I [insert positive opposite of the concern], how would I approach this?*

For example, if you suddenly worry you don't have enough resources to help you achieve your goals, ask yourself the questions, 'What steps could I take to make sure I have enough resources?' Or alternatively, 'If I knew I had all the resources I needed, how would I approach this?'

If you worry you don't have enough experience to do what you want to do, ask yourself, 'What steps can I take to make sure I have enough experience?' Alternatively, 'If I knew I had all the experience I needed, how would I approach this?'

When doubt kicks in you have to adjust your mindset to look for ways of overcoming limiting beliefs. We all have times when we are worried we might fail, but often the worry is more perception than reality. And the greatest determinant of success is the ability to push through this self-doubt.

Take control, adjust your perspective, open out your thinking and keep going.

## 4. Accept Accountability and Responsibility – Own and complete the activities

*No one gives you a break – you create breaks. You go out there and wrestle breaks to the ground and beat them into submission, you lure them out of their caves with sweets on a stick, you track them down and hunt them with an opportunity gun, you stay in their face until they give in – but no one gives them away.*

RICHARD TEMPLAR, AUTHOR, *THE RULES OF WEALTH*

You can have others help to hold you accountable to your goals and actions, and I would actively encourage it. But this should be secondary. You have to hold yourself accountable first. If you don't get it done, there will be no one else to blame but you.

In project management, two key terms are 'accountability' and 'responsibility'. The person accountable owns the project and the person responsible completes the project. However, in goal setting you have to be both, accountable for the ownership and responsible for its completion.

The extent to which you are willing to take accountability for your goal is directly proportional to the importance you place on the goal. If you aren't willing to hold yourself accountable then you need to re-asses the reason for the goal in the first place and the importance it holds for you. The 'why'.

Are you committed or not?

It's at times when you hit a bump in the road that accountability can dissolve a little, which is the reason the 'why' of goal setting is so important. If it matters enough, you'll find a way.

## 5. Know your plan – Actions to be established and completed over the short- and medium-term

*'Would you tell me please, which way I ought to go from here?' said Alice.*

*'That depends a good deal on where you want to get to,' said the Cat.*

*'I don't much care where...' said Alice.*

*'Then it doesn't matter which way you go,' said the Cat.*

LEWIS CARROLL, AUTHOR, *ALICE IN WONDERLAND*

Timelines will vary depending on your particular goal, but it often helps to break them down into more digestible pieces. As a rough estimate, your vision (or long-term goal) is likely to take between three and five years.

Your medium-term goals represent the milestones you need to reach in order to achieve the vision. So, if the long-term goal is to have completed a marathon in each of the seven continents over the next five years, you're going to need some milestones as to how you'll get there – and you'll need to get started in the next 12 months!

Finally, the short-term activities are the actions that build towards the achievement of your medium-term goals, which in turn build towards your long-term goals, or vision. The actions can normally be broken down into 90 days. Three months is a good amount of time: long enough to make progress and really achieve something, but not so long that you can't adjust or review your choices if needs be.

## 6. Establish a team – Ensure you have great people around you

*You can't stay in your corner of the
Forest waiting for people to come to you.
You have to go to them sometimes.*
A.A. MILNE, AUTHOR, *WINNIE THE POOH*

As part of your actions, you may need to consider who you need to involve. I mentioned the importance of opening up to people earlier, but this is slightly different. In the earlier section it was about sharing your hopes and dreams with people without expectation. At this point you should be reaching out to people you think can help in the achievement of your actions and goals.

So, what sort of people could you reach out to? Anyone who is able to augment the skills or knowledge you have today, or who can bring more to the table. It could be people who have an extensive network you can tap into; experts, or people who know experts in the area of your particular goal; people who have access to information; or who've been there and done what you want to do. Remember, success leaves clues so you don't have to reinvent the wheel. Find people who have already successfully done what you want to do and ask them for help.

## 7. Do It – Decide to start. Start now, follow up, review and adjust

*If you wait to do everything until you're sure it's right,*
*you'll probably never do much of anything.*
WINSTON BORDEN, AUTHOR AND POLITICIAN

There is something special and powerful that comes from starting – yet it is often the thing we find most difficult. We often put up barriers to beginning – some of them real, some of them perceived, but almost all surmountable.

Let's be clear, there is never a perfect time. Your plans will never be 100 percent perfect and you will never be totally ready – so don't set your expectations that high!

Just get started and adapt along the way if necessary.

### THERE'S NO BETTER TIME THAN NOW

When you look around at successful people, either those you know privately or those in the public eye, I can almost guarantee that they excel in this area and in all the elements in this chapter.

Being able to set goals and follow them through is a valuable skill. We all have the potential to set great goals and deliver on them, but too few people – in fact a minority – do. I said at the start of this chapter that too many people wake up every morning and start working from where they left off yesterday, without stopping to think or consider whether their activities are driving towards their goals.

It's not that they don't want or don't have goals, it's just that they lose focus or put up barriers. As you've seen, having a goal is one thing, but the most important element is defining 'why' you want it; after which there's another six steps to ensuring success. Sure, some people do them in a different order but the more of them you follow, the greater your chances of achieving success.

Within business and sales, the ability to set goals is crucial for both the long-term and medium-term. In addition, getting clear as to 'why' you get out of bed every morning can help bring clarity and motivation on those cold, early mornings when all you want is a day at home.

It also gives us the chance to make a difference to other people, through sharing your goals and letting them share theirs with you. In doing so, we can look for synergies, opportunities to collaborate and support with the combined desire to achieve. That's why this approach is different and why we need to *GO NAKED*.

It means stripping away the belief that in sharing our goals we'll put ourselves under undue pressure. It means tossing away the foolish belief that the person we tell will take our goal and achieve it first. We must shift our mindset to that of abundance. Having an abundant mindset means understanding that there is more than enough opportunity out there for all of us. The only caveat is this: it is reserved for those who go out and take it; for those who Get Clear, Open up, Never Doubt, are Accountable, Know Their Plan, Establish A Team and just Do It. It is reserved for those that *GO NAKED*.

# KEY MESSAGES

In order to Agree Goals:

- Develop an abundant mindset
- Understand 'adjusted reciprocity'
- Create your vision, goals and plans
    - Get Clear
    - Open Up
    - Never Doubt
    - Accept Accountability And Responsibility
    - Know Your Plan
    - Establish A Team
    - Do It
- Help others create their vision, goals and plans
- Agree your joint vision, goals and plans

# KEEP ADDING VALUE

*You can have everything in life you want, if you will just help other people get what they want.*
ZIG ZIGLAR, AUTHOR AND SPEAKER

## THE IDEA OF 'VALUE' AND 'SIGNIFICANCE'

An underlying theme that runs through *GO NAKED* is the belief that we have to be willing to open ourselves up to the world, that we can't operate or be successful in isolation. This applies to all aspects of our lives, but it is particularly important when we are building relationships with people. A great way to ensure you do this is to make it your mantra to 'keep adding value'.

The word 'value' is often used as a buzz word: people think it's something they should do, but with little or no understanding of what it actually means to add value. It sounds right, it sounds in vogue, but without being clear about what it means, and without taking steps towards doing so, it's just a nice sounding idea. However, it needs to be a promise and a personal commitment to which you will hold yourself accountable.

Another way of looking at value is in terms of *significance.* If we add value to people, we become significant. Similarly, every single person who is significant to us is, in some way, adding value to our lives. And so the closer our relationship with them, the greater our mutual contribution. Consider this: when you add significance, you create value; when you create value for others, you become more significant to them; and so the cycle continues.

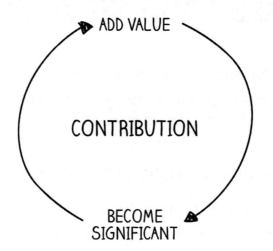

The reality is that there are so many people out there *taking* on a daily basis, rather than *giving,* that when someone arrives who wants to give the difference can be remarkable. They really stand out and it can become a point of differentiation. Of course, the great thing about adding value to others is that the more we focus on contributing in a worthwhile way to other people's lives, the more our own happiness becomes bound up with theirs. And it rarely costs us much more than our time and effort.

This principle can be applied to anyone. It could be friends, family, work colleagues or customers. It can determine how you act as a business person, business leader or in general day-to-day life. But in order to get people to believe in you, you have to add value in an authentic way. This can't be something you pretend to do or fake – you can't do it in your spare time. People can spot a fake a mile away, so you have to make yourself available to others and do it with genuine desire.

By now, I hope, you'll be starting to realise that the first step in *GO NAKED*, Getting Genuinely Curious, is a far-reaching concept and one that in itself can add value.

## Dental Options

Dr Barry Buckley is a dentist in Ireland. However, he's not just any dentist. He's one of the most successful dentists in Europe and runs Dental Options, a state of the art cosmetic dentistry suite in a private hospital outside Dublin. He and his network of dentists have also formed Clear Braces, one of the largest providers of the Invisalign system in Europe.

Ask Barry about why he's so successful, and this is what he'll tell you.

*We can never assume or infer to a potential patient that we know how they feel or think, because to do so is an invasion of privacy. It's an unsaid truth in today's overexposed market place that we are constantly assessing and evaluating prospective patients in a wide variety of ways; such as online polls and socio-demographic modeling. People can resent this – and rightly so. We have to treat our patients with 'actual' and not 'pretend' respect because we can no longer fake it. First and foremost, we have to show that we can add significance and value to our patients.*

How do Barry and his team add value first?

*We do so in what I would describe as both extrinsic and intrinsic ways.*

*Extrinsic refers to all the things that we can do for the patient that are not directly related to the teeth being treated. This might include: assistance with flexible working hours to facilitate their lifestyle; reminder texts for appointments; emailing or posting treatment plans; providing easy to read (in plain and easy to understand English) explanations of proposed treatment plans; a very informative and useful website; same day reply to email or phone requests; thank you letters; personalised Christmas cards with private messages; free whitening at special occasions (such as their children's wedding).*

*Intrinsic would involve everything related to the treatment that doesn't necessarily cost us much but means a lot... noise cancellation headphones; pain free anaesthesia; photographic software to give the patient an idea of what they will look like should they decide to go ahead with treatment; two consult appointments for the price of one – the first is to explore and the second to explain and plan; giving my private mobile number for emergency reasons; giving a lifetime warranty with all lab work; great support staff who can fully explain every treatment and options available.*

*Ultimately, giving patients choice is crucial and is the value they appreciate the most – the patient doesn't feel forced and feels you're on their side as you will happily do whichever treatment they choose.*

Now, I don't know about you, but to me that's a pretty impressive approach and one which, importantly, focuses on the patient first and offers immense value, therefore creating significance in the minds of the patients.

Why wouldn't you go there?

## YOU CAN'T TRICK THE LAW

We discussed the laws of 'adjusted reciprocity' earlier but a fundamental part of this is that you cannot 'trick' the law. In other words, you can't force it and you can't demand it. You'll often hear people say, 'I can't believe I did that for them and they gave me nothing in return.' Well, yes, that may be the case. But if you go through business and life doing things for other people in the hope and with the expectation that they will automatically give in return, you will be disappointed. Paradoxically, it is in adding value to others without expectation that we invoke the powers of 'adjusted reciprocity'.

Therefore, the other thing to keep in mind is that the value you receive may not come from the source you expect – from the person or person to whom you have created significance and given value. If adopting this approach is a universal one, in other words you do so indiscriminately, then you increase your reach and the value you receive may come from your broader social network.

## THREE RULES OF ADDING VALUE

Keep in mind three simple rules for this principle of value:

### 1. Give value first

Don't include yourself in the list of people who wait to receive before they give value. That's not how it works. You can't wait to see the good in someone else or wait until you've established whether you can profit from them before you act well towards them. Sorry, that just won't cut it.

### 2. Give value to as many people as possible

Do so universally and indiscriminately. People shouldn't fit into certain criteria – personal or professional – before you try to add significance. Just do it as often as possible to as many people as possible.

### 3. Give value without expectation

Don't expect anything in return, as if you do and it's not forthcoming, you'll feel disappointed and let down. Just do it because it's the right thing to do and let that provide the fulfillment you need. If you do it first, provide it to as many people as possible and do so without expectation, the rewards will be multiple times higher.

## DON'T LET SELLING BE A TRANSACTION

Remember this model from earlier? This is the traditional model of selling, which focuses on the transaction rather than on first adding value and creating significance.

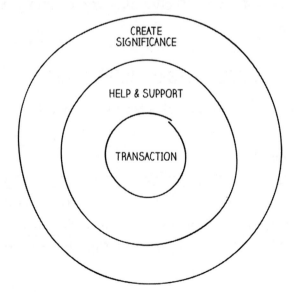

Selling can be merely a transaction – an act that is part of a process. But there can be a wide range of activity before the transaction and that's the important part. The sale itself should be secondary. Asking people to buy more just isn't going to work out in the long-run.

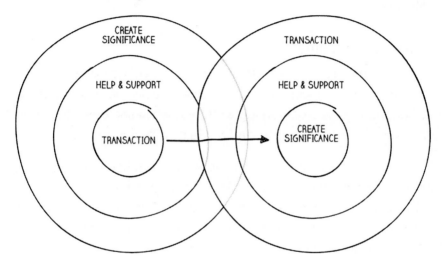

And this is the reason why adding value and creating significance is so important. Because it's what you do before the transaction of the sale itself which really matters. How can you better partner with your customers so that they truly value your time and input? How can you find ways to make a difference to them, and their business or institution? How can you find ways to ensure that you are the first person that they call when they need something? How can you ensure that you are front of mind when they want to buy?

The key is in the value or significance you bring to them. So find ways to add more value than the next person and you will unlock to the door to huge potential, personally and professionally. Focus on the sale and you will become another face in the crowd with little differentiation to separate you from the majority – the hordes of other sales people out there today, focusing on the end result rather than the journey.

Make it your business to do something every day for your customers.

## The path to recruitment

Michelle owns a recruitment firm in the UK, specialising in recruitment to the healthcare sector. She's easily the best recruiter I've had the pleasure of working with. And while she owns the company, she also takes the lead as Sales Director.

Michelle started the company 10 years ago from her spare bedroom. Today, her company is responsible for recruitment to some of the world's leading companies, some of them on an exclusive basis. In addition, over the last 10 years she has never had someone leave her business to go and work for a competitor.

What is it about Michelle that makes her so successful?

Michelle wanted to build a business based on relationships, on genuine relationships, with a view to being seen as a partner during the hiring process. She was determined to create value for her clients, sometimes by taking the less likely or more difficult route. Here is one such instance:

*In 2006 we were tasked with placing a senior role within a dental company. At the time, there was a candidate available with the right profile, who was also well known. In many ways there was an expectation that he would be on the shortlist. However, after speaking with him I just didn't feel he was the right fit for the company.*

*As I see it, part of our role in creating value is in making those decisions – in reducing the burden for the client, especially in senior roles and in those instances where we know the company well.*

*People don't want their time wasted, especially when they're busy and looking to fill an important role.*

*And so, as obvious as he was on paper, there was something which just didn't add up for me. Unlike other search agencies out there, I wasn't willing to put him forward just because he was available and well known. I was trying to create value and build trust.*

*Over the next few days, it became clear that although I hadn't put him forward, another agency had done.*

*The Managing Director of the client firm called me to express his disappointment at me not having selected him for interview. He was considering working with us on an exclusive basis and saw this as a real miss on our part. After all, he was an obvious candidate.*

*I told him that I just didn't feel he was the right fit for the company and that by not putting him through, I felt it would ultimately save him time, money and effort. I explained I wasn't in the business of sending through candidates where there would be an issue of alignment with the company's values.*

*After his interview with that candidate, the Managing Director called me. He had agreed that he wasn't the right fit. The interview had passed and there was no job offer. He thanked me for how I'd approached the situation on his behalf.*

Since then, Michelle has had exclusivity with that client for their recruitment. She attributes this to the fact that she did what was best for the client and not her bank balance; that she took a more difficult route and tried to create value first.

Michelle says, 'You can only get that kind of trust, in being the exclusive provider of recruitment services, by adding something of value to them and showing that you will provide a service that is free from just making a short-term gain or profit. That involves you proving to a customer that their needs are as important as yours.'

# 90 WAYS TO ADD VALUE STARTING TODAY

In order to get you started on your journey of value, significance and 'adjusted reciprocity', I'm going to provide you with a list of 90 ways in which you can add value to others every day. Why 90 ways? We talked in the previous chapter of the power of 90-day goals as an ideal time frame for taking action: long enough to see an impact; not so long that you can't change course after those 90 days if required. So, if the challenge is to make a difference over the next 90 days, you have 90 ways in which to do that and one of the actions can be to do something for someone else that adds value every day.

The options as to how you do this are endless. Here are 90 and there are countless more in your mind waiting to be unlocked. With the multitude of communication channels now available it's so easy for you to reach out to people. It wasn't so long ago that your options were limited to telephone, mail, a face-to-face visit or fax. Now you have email, SMS, YouTube, Twitter, LinkedIn, Facebook, Google+, Flickr, Instagram, WhatsApp; you can send them MP3s, MP4s, links to sites, podcasts and so much more. There are so many ways to connect. They key is using them and in a way which adds value. And if you really want to do something different you could always send a postcard, a letter or a fax!

Some of these ideas may resonate with you more than others. That's ok. Some may apply more to your personal life than professional life or vice versa. That's ok too. Their absolute applicability isn't what's key here. What is important is that you find your own ways in which to add value and significance to others. This list is my list and I hope it provides you with some inspiration and ideas of your own. The challenge is to create it and then live it out as best you can.

1. Acknowledge someone's accomplishments or achievements
2. Support someone in what they are doing
3. Offer to be available to someone when they need you
4. Challenge someone to be all that they can be
5. Assist someone without doing it for them
6. Motivate someone to teach others what they know
7. Let someone know how much they are appreciated
8. Give someone the credit they deserve
9. Help someone get clarity on their vision or long-term goal
10. Help someone to reach a goal
11. Help someone define actions required to achieve their goal
12. Share your own knowledge and understanding with someone
13. Share your own experiences with someone or share someone else's
14. Provide an additional or alternative perspective to someone
15. Actively listen to someone
16. Befriend someone regardless of their position or social status
17. Make someone laugh
18. Strive to really get to know someone
19. Teach someone a skill they do not have
20. Compliment someone just because you can
21. Compliment a person about something specific in front of another person
22. Ask someone a question about what interests them

23. Remember people's names

24. Remember people's anniversaries, and special occasions

25. Strive to be the first to help a person you know in need

26. Help people focus on their strengths

27. Help people in managing or negating their weaknesses

28. Find out what kinds of hobbies people have and send them articles, links, or ideas on the subject

29. Smile at people and smile when you talk

30. Say 'hello' to people when you walk by them

31. Express gratitude for the ways that people specifically add value to your life

32. Say 'please'

33. Say 'thank you'

34. When you learn something new, pass that information on to someone else

35. When someone asks for your help, do more than expected – go the extra mile

36. If you are going to an event, take someone with you

37. Pay for someone's lunch or dinner

38. Connect people who you think can benefit from each other

39. Offer to act as a sounding board to someone

40. Ask, 'Is there anything I can do to help you?'

41. Always bring something to the table – an opinion or idea

42. Highlight relevant opportunities

43. Share your knowledge with others. Don't keep your best ideas and strategies to yourself

44. Be honest with people – give them constructive feedback

45. Be open with someone about your shortcomings – you will make them feel more comfortable to share their own

46. 'Catch' somebody doing something right and recognise them for it

47. Help people find their niche or 'calling' in life

48. Encourage others

49. Refer business leads to others

50. Tell someone that you don't know something they do, and let them teach you

51. Hold others accountable to their commitments

52. Do unto others as you would have them do unto you

53. Challenge people and support their decision-making

54. Push people's comfort zones

55. When someone fails, encourage them to try again

56. Update someone on the latest industry trends

57. Update someone on the latest news

58. Update someone with articles related to their field of interest

59. Send links to videos or blogs

60. Update people on the latest product news

61. Update people on the latest promotions or offers

62. Offer someone a referral

63. Provide someone with networking opportunities

64. Provide information about a congress or education event

65. Give someone the opportunity to meet a key opinion leader or thought leader

66. Make yourself available to others

67. Send someone a postcard

68. Send them a birthday card

69. Just make them happier

70. Find a way to make a task easier for them

71. Send them interesting or relevant quotes

72. Help them make use of new technology

73. Share with them the latest relevant smartphone applications

74. Help others articulate their message or story

75. Help others to think more strategically

76. Use a story to help communicate a message

77. Translate or simplify complex information

78. Tell someone what others in a similar position have done

79. Offer to do something free of charge

80. Give a guarantee (for example, a money back guarantee)

81. Provide free education relevant to their interest

82. Write a blog

83. Give someone a book you think they'd like

84. Post comments on someone else's blog

85. Organise a party or other social event

86. Recommend someone

87. Send an unexpected gift

88. Help remove barriers or obstacles, perceived or real

89. Provide a reference for someone

90. Write someone a testimonial

## The Teacher and The Salesperson

Andrew Holliday is a teacher in Northumberland in the UK. He's a fantastic teacher. Not only does he genuinely care about his students, but he's also committed to making a difference every day. He could go and do other things but he chooses not to. He wants to teach. He's the first one in every day and the last one to leave. He runs clubs and events, hosts extra revision classes, raises money for the school and does far more than he needs to. As a result, he could walk into any school tomorrow and get a job.

Sheldon Krancher is a Salesperson, or a Territory Manager as he's known at Align Technology. I've never seen passion and enthusiasm like it for the product he sells. What's remarkable is that he sees more than just the product in what he does. In his mind, the product he sells makes a genuine difference to the lives of the people who use it. If you were selling the same product you might disagree; you might not see it the same way he does. But that's the beauty of it. He is unequivocal in his certainty that every day he is making a difference to his customers. He's been the top performing sales person in his organisation on more than one occasion.

All of the people in this chapter are real and they're still in their jobs today. For Barry, Michelle, Andrew and Sheldon, what makes them special is that they live out the following:

Action + Meaning = Significance

They all take action every day. They don't rest on their laurels, they don't get complacent and they don't take anything for granted. They keep working, keep going and try to be the best they can at whatever they do.

In addition, they believe that in their own way, big or small, what they're doing has meaning and that it makes a difference to other people. And they're right. Whether you or I or anyone else thinks what they do has any more or less meaning than the next person doesn't matter. They're clear in their mind.

As a result of this they create significance for the people around them: the patients they care for, the pupils they teach, the customers they serve. They're the best at what they do and successful in their own right.

Whatever you do, make it your goal to create significance for the people around you. Take action and do so with meaning.

## ADDING VALUE ISN'T ABOUT WINNING OR LOSING

Adding value isn't about winning or losing. It's not about being the best or the worst. There is no league table for it and no prizes at the end of the day. There's no first place.

It's an attitude, an approach – a way of life. It's about having an abundant mindset. And what I hope you've taken from this section is the positive impact that adding value can bring to you and others.

And if you've read this and thought, 'I already know this!'

Great.

But are you actually doing it, day in, day out?

If you are, please get in touch with me – I'd love to work with you.

If, like most of us, you do some of these things, some of the time, then make it your goal to do this more often, with more people, without expectation.

In many ways we aren't conditioned to add value to others over our formative years. Many of the experiences we have, and definitions of success we absorb, are based on looking out for number one – in school, in university, and in our jobs. We all have some degree of learned selfishness that means we want to live for ourselves and especially in today's get-rich-quick culture it's easy to think short-term and go for instant gratification. We may know that this isn't the best way to live, but we do so anyway because of the potential short-term impact. We don't do the things that add value and attract significance as much as we could as it takes us out of our comfort zone and into an area that feels strange, in which we feel vulnerable.

But think about what it means to GO NAKED – to lay yourself open, to push your comfort zone, to demonstrate vulnerability and strip away the layers that are superfluous to the building of strong, positive relationships. By finding ways to add value in the way that I've described, we do GO NAKED.

You will notice recurring themes as you move through the chapters and I hope that what you've read in this chapter reinforces the huge benefit of doing what has been described in the previous chapters. In being able to 'Get Genuinely Curious', 'Offer Something Different', 'Notice and Manage Yourself and Others' and 'Agree Goals' – and all of the components involved – you can genuinely add value to other people, whether in professional selling or any other context, to become a valued or trusted advisor.

When we create significance for other people, we in turn become more valuable. If you are an employee, find ways to become more valuable to your employer. If you own your own business, look for ways to create greater value for those you do business with. And think about your personal life and your closest relationships with your partner, parents, children, family or friends. How can you add more value for them and create even more significance? In doing so, notice the impact it has on you and the increase in your personal sense of satisfaction.

When we focus on creating significance and adding value to other people, and when we do so first, without expectation, it fundamentally changes our mindset. If we 'Keep Adding Value' as part of our efforts to *GO NAKED*, then the focus on success will become secondary and it will happen by default, as a result of our efforts.

## KEY MESSAGES

In order to Keep Adding Value:

- Understand the principles of value and creating significance
- Apply the three rules of adding value:
    - Give value first
    - Give value to as many people as possible
    - Give value without expectation
- Take action every day
- Use this list to create your own, to do something that adds value every day for the next 90 days

# EMBODY ENTHUSIASM

*Your work is going to fill a large part of your life, and the only way to be truly satisfied is to do what you believe is great work. And the only way to do great work is to love what you do. If you haven't found it yet, keep looking. Don't settle. As with all matters of the heart, you'll know when you find it.*

STEVE JOBS, CO-FOUNDER, CHAIRMAN AND CEO OF APPLE

## ENTHUSIASM IS IN DEMAND

We all know who these people are. They're the ones who have so much energy that when we're in their presence we feel energised. They talk with passion and excitement about their subject, and that in turn creates a synergistic effect – you feed off their energy, you in turn get excited – and it becomes a virtuous circle. They're great to be around and the time that you spend with them is enjoyable and effortless. You don't spend the time clock-watching and when you're with them the meeting or conversation passes quickly. When you realise how much time has passed it's a surprise.

Being in the presence of someone who has a real passion for what they do and an energy for life is a heartening experience. Often we find that we gain something just by being around them.

Think about the people you enjoy spending your time with. What are their characteristics? Would you describe enthusiasm as one of them?

The chances are that these people are great communicators and great influencers; that they are great at building relationships; and therefore the chances are that they're great at selling. It doesn't matter what it is that they're selling because with these people you really do end up buying based on the person.

Enthusiasm is important for many reasons, especially in developing great relationships. People generally are not attracted to and do not gravitate towards disinterested and apathetic people. In fact, we probably avoid them.

You know what it's like when you've been with someone who is negative in their outlook towards life. You walk away feeling drained, as if you've had all the energy and goodness sucked out of you. So, whilst enthusiasm can be a great tool for improving your own mindset, leveraging your enthusiasm can also be a great way to build relationships, create significance and step out from the majority.

However, enthusiasm isn't one dimensional and shouldn't be viewed as such. Don't think that excitement alone equals enthusiasm. It isn't about rushing headlong, out of control, with some reckless approach to life and it isn't a cavalier approach to situations that diminishes the need for a considered plan of action.

## The excited salesman

A new vacuum cleaner salesman knocked on the door of the first house of the street. He had been perfecting a new sales pitch and couldn't wait to try it out. This one was fool-proof!

A lady answered the door.

Before she could speak, the excited salesman barged into the living room, opened a big black plastic bag and poured manure all over the carpet.

'Madam, if I can't clean this up with the use of this new powerful vacuum cleaner, I will eat all of this s...!' he exclaimed.

'Would you prefer chili sauce or ketchup with that?' asked the lady.

The bewildered salesman, knocked off his stride, asked, 'Why, madam?'

'Because,' replied the lady, 'there is no electricity in the house.'

# THE ENTHUSIASM FORMULA

Enthusiasm is multi-faceted and, to be at its most effective, includes three elements: interest, knowledge and mindset.

$$Interest + Knowledge \times Mindset = Enthusiasm$$

Importantly, enthusiasm is as much about your mindset as anything else. It's certainly the multiplier in the equation and has far greater influence than the other elements. It determines how you're willing to approach a situation and drives whether you have an empowering mindset or a disempowering mindset. In other words, do you see things positively or negatively, constructively or destructively?

## Interest

There has to be an inherent belief in what you do. This cannot be faked – not in the long-term. And even if you could fake it successfully, the tension created would probably be too much to bear. There has to be a genuine love or interest, (or a Genuine Curiosity), in the person or subject. When you are genuinely interested in someone else, you cut out the surrounding noise and focus on the individual. This is the same type of interest: focused and deliberate.

## Knowledge

When you're enthusiastic you want to know more, you want to learn more and you want to gain as much knowledge in your subject as possible. Therefore, having a deep knowledge comes from enthusiasm and also creates more enthusiasm. This in turn breeds credibility. You become someone who is not only passionate about their chosen subject, but also very knowledgeable and believable.

## Mindset

The third element is mindset. You have to believe in what you're doing. You have to feel like you're making a difference and that what you are passionate about is worth your enthusiasm and involvement. This inner belief manifests itself as confidence and helps cultivate belief in the minds of others. Mindset is the multiplier.

Great sales people, great influencers and great communicators are deeply passionate about what they do. They don't have to be, they just are. If you give some thought to people you know who have this characteristic, you'll realise they have a number of things in common.

## LEVERAGING INTEREST AND KNOWLEDGE

Interest and Knowledge go hand in hand. If you're interested in something, it makes you keener to learn about it; your additional knowledge feeds your interest and it's another virtuous circle.

Consider this diagram, with respect to your approach to work, life or a chosen subject.

Which quadrant do you sit in today?

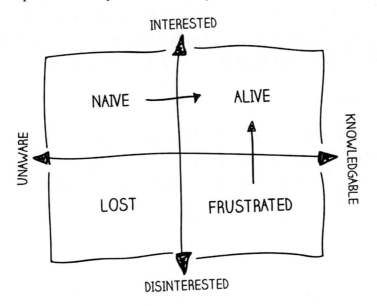

If you're in the bottom right quarter, you're knowledgeable about your particular subject, but lacking interest. This leads to 'frustration'. It may mean you are in the wrong job: you could be well trained, capable or tenured, but inherently lacking interest in what you do. So something needs to change and that change needs to lead to a greater level of interest. Once you combine the two, you become 'alive'.

If you're in the top left, you are interested in what you do, but lack the necessary knowledge. You could be described as 'naïve' in that area. This might be the case when you are starting a new course, a new job or a new project. This is the easiest gap to bridge, because change is down to you and within your control. How can you become more knowledgeable and leverage your interest?

If you're able to combine knowledge and interest you can generate excitement and you feel 'alive'. This is the top right quadrant. What you do with that excitement and how you turn it into enthusiasm will be conveyed through your behaviour; people who get this right step away from the majority.

A note about the bottom-left hand corner:

If for any reason you're in this quadrant, you're 'lost' and something needs to change. Lost can quickly turn to despair. You must do something to increase your knowledge, your interest or both. This is not a sustainable place to be.

# CHILD'S PLAY

I can't help but be amazed at my two young children and how they start each day. They always have so much excitement and eagerness for the day. They smile as if they haven't seen you in weeks and the look on their faces tells you they're genuinely excited about the day ahead.

And it doesn't end there. From beginning the day with the greatest excitement, they then approach everything with absolute curiosity and wonder. They treat everything as if it is brand new: inside or outside; in books or on TV; animals, toys, cars, planes – everything.

They're not anxious, they have an unshakeable sense of security and they bring endless energy to their play.

But things change as we grow older. We become more aware of our environment and the factors that influence us daily. We become more impacted by what goes on outside of us and our mindset can become influenced by our surroundings.

We can learn from a child's approach to their day. If we were to begin each day with excitement and eagerness; if we were to be curious and questioning; if we didn't worry and lived with a sense of inner security; how would that impact our lives?

Enthusiasm means throwing ourselves into a relationship, goal, dream, or activity. It means casting aside worries or distractions and embracing instead the delights of the moment or the hope of success. Enthusiasm makes us feel fully alive and comes from how we think and feel inside, not what goes on around us. Enthusiasm is child's play.

## THE BEHAVIOUR OF THE ENTHUSIAST

*If you want to be enthusiastic, act enthusiastic.*
DALE CARNEGIE, AUTHOR AND LECTURER

Let's look at what makes enthusiastic people the way they are and consider how that relates to us. The third element within the equation – the multiplier – is mindset. How does that manifest itself; what are the behaviours that create its multiplying effect and generate enthusiasm?

We can all think of times when we were really enthusiastic about something – so much so that we were filled with the feeling and couldn't hide it.

Take some time to think about that experience, how you felt at the time, and try to recreate it in your mind's eye.

What are the behaviours we exhibit when we're enthusiastic about something?

### PASSION

Enthusiastic people have a passion for what they do. It's why they get up in the morning – often early! They're excited about it and want to tell you. They have a desire for it and aren't easily dissuaded from it.

*When we're enthusiastic about something, we act with passion.*

## LANGUAGE

Think about the language that enthusiastic people use. They choose their words carefully – it may not be obvious at first, but listen. Seldom will you hear them using negative or dull language. What they say is positive and upbeat; it has a rhythm and spring to it.

*When we're enthusiastic about something, our language becomes much more positive.*

## PACE

Enthusiastic people move with pace. If they say they're going to do something, they do it. If there is a task to be done, they offer to do it. They do it quickly, and they do it well. They're often busy, but rarely do you hear them say, 'I'll put that off for another day.' They don't procrastinate. They're satisfied with 90 percent rather than 100 percent if it means getting the job done.

*When we're enthusiastic about something, we move quickly and act with pace.*

## RELATIONSHIPS

Enthusiastic people tend to have great relationships, which have both breadth and depth. They're relaxed and easy-going. They're not uptight or highly strung. They make people feel at ease. They can adjust their behaviour to the person, putting them at ease, and to the situation, which allows them to resonate with different people.

*When we're enthusiastic about something, we develop great relationships.*

## NEW OPPORTUNITIES

Not surprisingly, enthusiastic people are also receptive to new opportunities. If someone offers them the chance to be part of something, more often than not they say 'yes'. They don't keep themselves to themselves and they're willing to get involved. They understand that although not everything will work out every time, new opportunities will arise if they're willing to make themselves available. They don't worry that they may fail, or that it may not bring them great results. They just give it a go and enjoy the experience.

*When we're enthusiastic about something, we say 'yes' to new opportunities.*

## INVOLVE OTHER PEOPLE

Enthusiastic people tend to have great people around them. It's easy to understand why – they attract them like a magnet. People want to spend their time with enthusiastic people because it's contagious. Moreover, they actively seek out great people to have around them. They aren't scared of sharing ideas and they only see benefit in doing so.

*When we're enthusiastic about something, we involve other people.*

## HUMOUR

If you're enthusiastic, you have a smile on your face. You laugh with people and you laugh at yourself. You don't take yourself too seriously because you're not preoccupied or on edge. You're focused on what it is you're enthusiastic about, and you're great to be around.

*When we're enthusiastic about something, we laugh.*

## PRAGMATISM

There are things you can control and things you can't. Enthusiastic people focus on the things that they can control. They don't stress or worry about the things they have little or no influence over or the things that they can't control.

*When we're enthusiastic about something, we focus on the things we can control.*

## KINDNESS

Enthusiastic people tend to be kind. Why? Because they are filled with a positive energy, which makes them want to do something for other people. Not for any particular reason and not with the expectation of anything in return. They add value to others and do it just because they can.

*When we're enthusiastic about something, we're kind to others.*

## LET GO

We all experience bumps in the road – bad, upsetting or disappointing experiences. Enthusiastic people don't dwell on them. They don't live in the past. They don't hold grudges and they're not resentful.

*When we're enthusiastic about something, we let go of the past.*

## AVOID NEGATIVITY

Enthusiastic people don't listen to the naysayers. They don't listen to the people who criticise without being constructive or seem to be focused on negativity. They aren't discouraged and keep going.

*When we're enthusiastic about something, we aren't easily detracted from our goal.*

## GRATEFUL

When we're enthusiastic about something, we're grateful. Grateful for the opportunity, grateful for the experience and grateful for what we have. This attitude leads to enjoyment and further enthusiasm.

*When we're enthusiastic about something, we're grateful.*

You may be able to think of other common traits you have when you feel enthusiasm or that you see in enthusiastic people you know. These are some of the outstanding ones that make those people what they are.

So the question is this: if we know that these are the behaviours we observe in enthusiastic people; if we know that these are the behaviours we demonstrate when we're enthusiastic about something, how can we better leverage this information?

For each of these contributing factors, think about the actions you could take in order to amplify how you demonstrate them. What can you do to live with more passion, use more positive language or act with more pace? How can you go out and build new relationships? What new things can you try or new opportunities can you say 'yes' to? How can you start to involve more people more often? Can you laugh more frequently? How can you start to focus on those things within your sphere of control versus those which aren't? What steps can you take to demonstrate kindness to others? What is there from your past which you need to just let go? How can you be more robust against the negativity that sometimes comes from others? How can you be more grateful for what you have?

## THE HAPPINESS ADVANTAGE

Shawn Achor is the founder and CEO of Good Think Inc, and his book, *The Happiness Advantage*, looks at the conventional formula that in order to be happy we have to be successful – and turns it on its head. His research suggests that in order to be successful we should focus on being happy first.

In his book, he states that our traditional approach to happiness is based on a belief that that we will be happy once we are successful. For instance, if we're in school then we say we'll be happy once we get a place in university – and then we get the place. But we're not happy because next we want to graduate with a good degree. We do that, but still we're not happy because what we really want is a good job – and if we just get that job, then we'll be happy. Of course we get a job, but then we want more – a better job, promotion or a raise. And we never reach that state of happiness because we keep changing what our definition of success looks like; what our definition of happiness is. The goal posts keep moving.

Shawn's thesis is that, if on the other hand we focus on being happy with our lives first, we are more likely to achieve successful outcomes. He suggests that every single relationship, business and educational outcome improves when the brain is positive first. (You can find his talk on Ted.com for a beautiful summary of this.)

In many ways, I see enthusiasm as the same as happiness. In other words, enthusiasm and success also go hand in hand, but enthusiasm comes first. Don't wait to be successful. Don't say, 'I'll be enthusiastic when I get the sale, the job or the promotion.'

Just get enthusiastic. Because enthusiasm inspires confidence and raises morale. Enthusiasm comes from the inside out and it's a state we can develop. So, as with the Happiness Advantage, rather than focus on success, focus first on being enthusiastic.

## Meet Isaiah

Meet Isaiah Hankel. In 2011, Isaiah graduated from the University of Iowa with a PhD in Anatomy and Cell Biology. Since then he's been working as a biomedical consultant full time. However, Isaiah is also an author and serial entrepreneur.

Over the past two years, Isaiah has launched three online products, consulted for 12 different companies, and has given over 250 seminars in 20 different countries through Europe, New Zealand, Australia and North America. In 2012, Isaiah founded Cheeky Scientist, a networking platform for entrepreneurs and people earning and holding advanced degrees and in 2014 he will publish his first book.

If you visit his site, http://www.isaiahhankel.com, you can read testimonials and watch numerous videos of Isaiah in action. When you do this, one thing becomes clear: Isaiah embodies enthusiasm. It flows from him naturally and transmits to other people, whether you're watching his videos or talking to him in person.

Because of this, two things happen. First, you can't help but be impacted by him. Some of his ideas will resonate with you more than others, of course, but his ability to influence is far greater than it otherwise would be. Second, you become interested – interested to find out more.

As a result, he has established an international networking platform, sells a range of online products and has over 15,000 people reading his articles every week.

What a great position to be in. To be able to impact people and spark their interest.

Now, to be fair, Isaiah has a PhD so he's bright and his ideas have substance. But substance without enthusiasm would be like having the most beautiful car you can imagine but without any fuel. Enthusiasm is the fuel. It fuels Isaiah and it can fuel you and the people around you too.

## ENTHUSIASM WINS

When you have two people, two ideas, two businesses that are equally matched, enthusiasm can make the difference. When you're not sure which way to go, enthusiasm can be the deciding factor as enthusiasm inspires and motivates people.

In order to inspire people, in order to communicate with passion, in order to develop great relationships and in order to sell successfully, you have to be enthusiastic. Enthusiasm can be cultivated, nurtured and developed. We can all take steps to be more enthusiastic. However, the underlying requirement is that you have to believe in what you're doing.

Harry Truman, the 33rd President of the United States said, 'I studied the lives of great men and famous women, and I found that the men and women who got to the top were those who did the jobs they had in hand, with everything they had of energy and enthusiasm.'

Great sales people are enthusiastic, they have a passion for what they do and they believe in what they do. In the context of *GO NAKED*, enthusiasm means throwing ourselves into relationships, goals, dreams or activities. It means casting aside worries or distractions and embracing instead the delights of the moment or the hope of success. It means being authentic and not afraid to show our excitement.

Enthusiasm is the energy that drives successful results. If we want to accomplish great things; if we want to realise great goals; if we want to step out from the majority and to live a great life, we absolutely must possess enthusiasm for what we do. Enthusiasm helps us attract those things we desire and it makes us more attractive to others too.

## KEY MESSAGES

In order to Embody Enthusiasm:

- Understand the Enthusiasm formula:
    - Interest + Knowledge x Mindset = Enthusiasm
- Model the behaviour of the enthusiast
    - Live with passion
    - Use positive language
    - Act with pace
    - Develop great relationships
    - Say 'yes' to new opportunities
    - Involve other people
    - Laugh
    - Focus on what is in your control
    - Act with kindness
    - Let go of the past
    - Avoid negativity
    - Be grateful
- Apply the happiness advantage – focus on being enthusiastic first

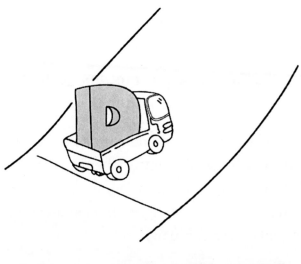

# DO IT AND DELIVER

*People may doubt what you say;*
*but they will believe what you do.*
LEWIS CASS, MILITARY OFFICER AND POLITICIAN

## HOW DO YOU WANT TO BE REMEMBERED?

Do you want to be known as someone who was 'all talk and no action'? Someone who 'talked a good game'? Do you want to be thought of as unreliable? Do you want to be recalled as a bit of a let-down?

I imagine, in fact I know, that the answer to all of these questions is an unequivocal 'no'.

So let's split this principle into two components:

**PART 1 – DO IT:** For yourself. In other words, taking action, taking a risk and being proactive

**PART 2 – DELIVER:** For others. Put differently, keeping your word and delivering on your promises

The extent to which you can demonstrate both of these components can make a huge difference when it comes to business, relationships and selling. In addition, it can determine the extent to which someone is willing to do business with you, both as an individual or as a company.

Think about the hours spent and the money invested in training people to improve certain skills or behave in a particular way. Then the biggest issue business owners and executives face is ensuring that people actually take action.

It's essential because it's these basics, these fundamentals which can dramatically influence the degree of success we may or may not achieve. And without this step, everything else becomes redundant. This final principle is the engine that powers the different facets of *GO NAKED*.

# PART 1 – DO IT

## Taking action, taking a risk and being proactive

Look at the best sales people out there. Look at the most successful people out there. You see people who commit to doing something, to taking action, and then actually doing it. They don't just
talk about it and postulate their planned success – they actually
do something about it. They believe that actions speak louder
than words and they are focused on actually doing. When they
commit to something for themselves or for other people, they
don't differentiate between the two. Either way, it's a personal
commitment and one they hold themselves accountable to.

## No, there will never be a perfect time

In 2008, in the midst of the worst financial crisis in living memory,
Parminder Basran left his well-paid job in his family business to
move to London and begin his MBA at London Business School.
Many thought he was crazy; they couldn't understand what he was
gaining by going back to school.

Two years later he graduated from London Business School and,
with the economy still in tatters, he set up his own business, Twenty
Ten Capital, a mid-market private equity fund. Again, the doubters
told him he was mad to do so, but he persisted.

Now, less than three years later, his business is flourishing. Today
he's got offices in London, Singapore and Ibiza; has executed five
private equity transactions and has exited one of those; he's never
looked back. Ask him about what he does and he'll tell you, 'It's the
next best thing to being a professional footballer or a rock star!' The
naysayers are left despondent while Parminder and his business
move from strength to strength.

## Why don't we just jump?

All too often we don't jump and, as a result, there are too many people with a lot to give whose ideas and creativity never get to see the light of day. They're kept locked away in the recesses of their mind until the time is right, when the time is perfect.

As much as they may long for that ideal moment, there will never be a perfect time.

There are a many reasons why we stall and don't jump, but many of them are based on myths. Whilst each of them may feel real in the moment, most of them lack substance and are issues of perception rather than reality.

So, what are some of the reasons why we don't start? What are the reasons there aren't more people like Parminder?

### BECAUSE WE'RE WAITING FOR MORE

We don't start because we put barriers in our way and claim, *'I'll start when…':*

*'I'll start when I've got more capital.'*

*'I'll start when I've got more experience.'*

*'I'll start when I have more people/the right people in my network.'*

*'I'll start when I have more time.'*

Ask someone who makes such statements what they would do with the extra capital if they had it, or how much they would specifically need and there will be no detailed or substantive response; ask how much more experience is required to ensure success and you hear uncertainty and  open-ended timelines;

ask them how many more people they need in their network and it's always more than they've got, but no clear plans of how to acquire them; ask someone who tells you they need more time whether they could free up that time now, and the answer is negative – it becomes evident that the problem isn't one of time but prioritisation.

It's always possible to create more of any of these resources at a future point in time. However, not having more today can be a poor reason not to start. Ironically, abundance in any of these areas can be created once the decision has been made to start.

Start now and you'll generate more revenue; start now and you'll gain experience along the way; start now and you'll build your network; start now and it will become important enough to create the time.

### BECAUSE WE THINK WE NEED A 100 PERCENT DEFINED, INDESTRUCTIBLE, BULLET PROOF PLAN

It's nice to feel safe. When you've got a plan you feel safe. When someone gives you a plan you feel even safer. When someone gives you their plan, tells you to go and do it, they take responsibility for it and it feels safer still. 'Here, follow these steps – you can't fail – and even if you do, I'll catch you.'

It's happened to all of us and it can feel comfortable – restrictively so. We've been given the plan, the way forward, the 'task list' to get something done. We haven't had to question it, just execute it, without stopping to think whether it was good, bad or average. But there's no perfect plan. Only 'good enough' for now and 'good enough' to get started.

If you're going to jump it's going to have to be *your* plan. Yes, you can ask for help and support, but you're going to need to take responsibility. No strategy is bullet-proof, a 'dead cert' rarely exists and plans are malleable. That's the beauty, though: learn whilst you go and adapt as necessary.

## BECAUSE WE'RE WAITING FOR PERMISSION

We've been told to get in line and wait. We've been told we need permission to get going. This, despite the fact that we are living in an era when companies are crying out for creativity; when countless products are being commodified; when the race to the bottom is more often run than the race to the top; when a business can be started with little or no capital; and when standing out can have huge impact for the individual and the company.

The truth is, you don't need someone more senior than you in the room to create ideas; you don't need to be asked to come to the table with something new that you believe can change the landscape; and you don't need permission to start something which you have faith in.

Fortune favours the brave and sometimes it's better to ask forgiveness than to ask for permission.

## BECAUSE WE THINK THAT IT'S NOT FOR 'PEOPLE LIKE US'

We have to lose the mindset that success in any field isn't for people like us, as if it's reserved for an elite few. If we don't lose that mindset we automatically assume that starting, jumping, isn't for 'people like us': if we didn't go to the right school, the right university, come from the right place or family, had the right job or experience we're out of contention and the privilege is reserved for people who fit with our ideals.

But that thinking is a myth. The opportunities in front of you today are available for people like you. The only question is whether you are willing to take them or not. And that bears no correlation to your external environment or conditions but to your mindset and ability to get started.

As David Mamet, the American playwright said, 'You are not one of the myriad of interchangeable pieces, but a unique human being, and if you've got something to say, say it and think well of yourself whilst you're learning to say it better.'

This view is an empowering one and gives you permission, if you need permission, to start and do it better along the way. Because of course there will never be a perfect time to have a go at something new, especially if it's something that requires a significant change. And this isn't to underestimate what is required, because at times it can be tough, but something special happens when you just get going. The energy and the momentum that results can do wonders and allow you to achieve more – to jump higher and further – than you ever thought possible.

To GO NAKED is to take action today – to not wait, or put off for the future, but to start now. To embrace the fear that sometimes enmeshes us, knowing that the time might not be perfect or the idea exactly right, but that it's ok. Because history tells us that the timing was never perfect for other people either. Sometimes we need a cliff to jump off. We need to stand there and look down and know we only have one option. Stepping back from the brink is not it. The only way is to go forwards and jump.

Whatever you want to do, whatever you've been waiting to start, whatever you've been putting off – just start. Do it.

You can do any of the things you've considered but not yet started. The only choice is whether you really want to. Once you've made the decision and committed, the rest will start to fall into place. You have no idea what you could create – your best piece of work yet could be just over that cliff.

## PART 2 – DELIVER

### Keeping your word and delivering on your promises

Keeping your word is one of the most effective ways of earning the respect of others and building a solid reputation, both personally and professionally. Although it seems such a simple concept, that should in no way undermine its critical nature.

The world is littered with broken promises, and with them the remains of relationships that were damaged in the process.

Customers want accessibility and reliability. In other words, they want to be able to call on you when they need you and for you to do what you say you will. Therefore, start simply by doing what you say you will and making yourself accessible. The quicker people realise that they can call you and you will do what you say you will, the sooner business will start to flourish. Remember, your word is your reputation, so protect it. Keep your word and people will keep you.

If we want to have a solid relationship based on trust, we have to be consistent and we have to behave in ways that engender trust. *GO NAKED* is about demonstrating vulnerability – but it has to work both ways. If we want the other person to open up and to let their guard down and risk being vulnerable, they have to trust us. Honoring your word plays a powerful role in building this trust and in impacting how you are viewed by others. In the longer-term, it also plays a large part in how you view yourself. If keeping your word and delivering on promises demonstrates a respect for others, by the same token it also shows a level of respect for yourself.

## Standing Out

It is often so hard to differentiate ourselves in the marketplace today and it may become increasingly more difficult to stand out from the majority. This applies to products and services but, perhaps even more importantly, it applies to the people who work and interact with customers. It applies to you and me.

So how can you make a difference? How can you stand out?

One simple way is to do what you say you will for others – with immediate follow up and moving through to completion as soon as possible. Follow up means confirming the agreed actions with them immediately after leaving them, and completion means ensuring that the specific actions are delivered within the agreed timeframe.

This appears simple and it is.

But it's not done routinely and people are missing a trick. I guarantee that if it is done consistently, you can easily differentiate yourself from others. The fact is there's absolutely no reason why it shouldn't be done 100 percent of the time.

How can this help you stand out? When you commit to doing something then deliver on it you build three important elements:

### 1. TRUST

People see you as being reliable and someone they can turn to. When something needs to be done or when an opportunity arises they will look to you and not your competitor. After all, people want to work with people they can trust.

### 2. CREDIBILITY

When people experience you doing what you say you will, their level of confidence in you increases. Confidence breeds credibility, and opportunities to become more significant come your way.

### 3. MOMENTUM

Momentum and pace become a habit. You can move from one thing to another with ease and handle greater complexity. You do things more effectively and with greater impact. It becomes a virtuous cycle.

The next time you leave someone with an agreed set of actions, whether a customer or a colleague, follow up with them immediately to confirm the agreed actions and then commit yourself to completing them within the agreed timeframe. Build trust, build credibility and use momentum as your vehicle.

It's the little things which can allow you to stand out and make a difference, and this can be one of them.

## I know it's obvious

But let's face it, 99 percent of people are good people and they don't set out to diminish trust in them through not doing what they said they would. On the contrary, they would probably be mortified that they were viewed in that way. Often it just comes down to carelessness: carelessness in the way that they discuss and agree desired outcomes; carelessness in the way they set expectations; and, finally, lacking the personal accountability for the delivery of whatever they committed to.

## Discuss and agree desired outcomes

One of the key principles we looked at earlier was that goals should be agreed. In similar fashion, the commitments or promises that we make should also be discussed and agreed in the context of the planned goal. Doing so means both parties have 'skin in the game'; both parties have a set of actions which, when executed, should lead to a successful outcome.

A common mistake is not to discuss and agree these outcomes up front. It isn't clear what the end goal is and why the actions, on either side, are contributing towards that goal. A lack of purpose results, as does a lack of 'why' and a lack of accountability; it therefore becomes too easy for the actions to fall by the wayside. But this is GO NAKED, so those goals and dreams should be shared, they should be discussed and joint goals should be planned. We should be willing to take the risk of holding ourselves accountable, and in discussing and agreeing the desired outcomes we are making a conscious decision to take action towards them.

Another way of looking at this is that commitments shouldn't be made in isolation. They should be part of an integrated approach in which each party is clear on both the outcome, the deliverables along the way, the responsibilities and the timelines. This greatly increases the chances of the actions being executed, as we are all bought into the 'reasons why'.

## Set expectations

If you're not going to do something immediately or within a given time frame, make that clear. One of the biggest causes of frustration is lack of communication on this subject. It has less to do with someone deliberately not doing something, and more with a lack of common understanding and agreement about the timelines by which something should be done. This links back to the need to discuss and agree desired outcomes.

The need to 'Agree Goals' is also crucial as a distinct step within GO NAKED, but also helpful within this section. The same can be said for the need to 'Offer Something Different'. The ability to be able to challenge thinking plays a part in many steps during relationship development, but none more important than when agreeing what the actions should be. At this point, we can challenge whether or not the suggested next steps are really the ones that will create the biggest impact.

Sometimes particular actions or activities carry more urgency with one person than they do with another. The difference in perception of importance, combined with different people being responsible for delivery, causes problems if not communicated effectively. So we have to discuss and agree desired outcomes linked to the overarching goals; we have to challenge assumptions and challenge what will really make the biggest difference; and we have to commit to them being done.

A common phrase is to 'under-promise and over-deliver', and if this works for you, fine. But it's more about being clear as to who will do what and when.

## Make it personal

Ultimately, you have to care and, in addition, you have to understand that perception is reality and that others will not make a distinction between your willingness and ability to deliver on your promises and 'you'. It takes more time and emotional energy to repair a damaged relationship after a shirked commitment than it does to keep it. Keeping our word is not only about respecting others but about respecting ourselves too.

If you follow this, you're holding yourself accountable to the most important person you can – you. When you have an agreed action to carry out, don't just make it another 'to do' as part of a long and ever growing list. If you are committed to it, make it a 'must do'.

## It's not what you say, but what you do

It's not what a person tells you that matters. It's how they treat you that reveals their true feelings and beliefs. Their character is revealed not by the promises they make, but the promises they keep.

The biggest issues in this area come from a lack of communication – in failing to discuss and agree desired outcomes and in failing to set expectations. As I said, 99 percent of people are good people who only have good intentions. But their inability to do what they say they will comes down to a failure in one of these two areas, if not both. And sometimes, in their desire to please or be liked, they shoot too high – way too high – in their commitments, to a level that they could never achieve. But others don't care about that and they still hold them to the same standards. And then frustration kicks in.

This is why it is crucial that you take time to openly communicate with the other person – about their 'why', their goals and the actions along the way. If you do so, not only do you improve the chances that the decisions taken in pursuit of the goals will be the right ones, but that you are both clear on the manner and the time in which they will be delivered.

In trying to build relationships based on the principles discussed through this book, there is a series of common links between all the different elements. To be open, to do things which engender trust, which allow people to feel comfortable to open up, to lay themselves bare and to be able to demonstrate vulnerability. These elements have been consistent throughout GO NAKED and, in this section, it is about taking on responsibility and accountability to get things done. You're taking it personally.

In order to accomplish these things and beat the majority, we have to show that we can be that person. That we are worthy of the other person's trust and can not only play the part but live it out authentically. Nothing diminishes trust so much as a series of broken promises or commitments. That's why this step is so important: without the right level of attention to this, the rest of the good work will go to waste. You can do all the other things – Get Genuinely Curious, Offer Something Different, Agree Goals, Keep Adding Value and Embody Enthusiasm – but fail to deliver on a series of commitments and promises and this all breaks down.

To *GO NAKED* you have to demonstrate these qualities and show the other person that they can put their faith and trust in you. In doing so, your relationships will be more mutually beneficial than you could ever have envisaged.

## KEY MESSAGES

- Do it – with respect to yourself
  - o Know that there is never a perfect time
    - ▪ That you will never have a bullet proof plan
    - ▪ That you don't need to wait for permission
    - ▪ And that people 'like you' can do it
- Deliver – with respect to others
  - o Do what you say you will
    - ▪ With immediate follow up and through to completion
    - ▪ Which builds trust, credibility and momentum
  - o Discuss and agree desired outcomes
  - o Set expectations
  - o Make it personal

# WHAT DOES IT MEAN TO 'GO NAKED'?

*When we were children, we used to think*
*that when we were grown-up we would no*
*longer be vulnerable. But to grow up is to accept*
*vulnerability. To be alive is to be vulnerable.*
MADELEINE L'ENGLE, AUTHOR

As you read through the chapters of *GO NAKED*, you will find seven interconnecting principles which, if followed, will allow you to build stronger relationships, in sales, business and in life.

The theme which runs through all these steps and ideas is a one of being *naked*, so I want to spend some time providing a little more detail about why this principle and the idea of being naked is so important.

## THE REALITY TV CULTURE

It's so easy for us, especially today, to try and adopt a certain set of behaviours which, in many ways, aren't really ours or representative of us. Whether in business or in life, it's easy to adopt a façade which is linked either to a set of learned behaviours or those traits which we believe will make us better, more attractive or more successful. Perhaps it's as a result of our get-rich-quick, *X-Factor*-influenced culture; or perhaps it's as a consequence of us striving for success and believing that it will only be available under certain conditions or through a certain representation of us.

Every day, we see people who, rather than being the authentic person they really are, adopt such a façade and act out their time with others as the person they *think* they should be rather than the person they are. We see people who aren't as honest with themselves or others and therefore fail to take responsibility. All too often, we see instances where, if people were brave and took action, they would genuinely improve their chances of success, but instead they worry about the consequences of moving rather than of standing still. We see too many examples of people unwilling to ask for help for fear that it may be perceived as a sign of weakness or being afraid that that the answer will be 'no' and that they'll be rejected. Finally, and perhaps too often, we see a lack of humility in the fact that most of our choices are half chance.

These are the people who form the majority.

But there is another way.

We can strip away all of these layers, the façade, the learned behaviours, the negative behaviours; we can take down our masks and we can show the real us; we can be proud of what we are, who we are and be willing to take responsibility for ourselves. To do so means to act with vulnerability, and this is what it means to *GO NAKED*.

*To share your weakness is to make yourself vulnerable;*
*to make yourself vulnerable is to show your strength.*

CRISS JAMI, POET, PHILOSOPHER AND DESIGNER

Throughout the book, we've looked at the principles which can allow us to *GO NAKED* – to Get Genuinely Curious, to Offer Something Different, to Notice and Manage Yourself and Others, to Agree Goals, to Keep Adding Value, to Embody Enthusiasm, and to Do It And Deliver. And running through each of these principles, to fully live in this way, requires a willingness to do so in a *naked* way.

The following components are those which I believe should provide the context for each of the principles. In other words, they should fuel the process. For each of the principles this fuel should run through and power the components within each one. Get these ideas right and the rest will follow.

## BE AUTHENTIC

*There is nothing more beautiful than*
*seeing a person being themselves. Imagine going*
*through your day being unapologetically you.*

STEVE MARABOLI, *LIFE, THE TRUTH, AND BEING FREE*
– SPEAKER, AUTHOR AND BROADCASTER

At the heart of being naked is the willingness to accept yourself and be true to your own personality, spirit or character. This is despite any external pressures which have the potential to influence you on a day-to-day basis. So it's about being the person that is uniquely 'you' and not the one defined by your role or job. It removes the need for some kind of image management and actually says, 'I'm ok with whom I am.' When you see these people, they tend to shine and inspire.

## BE HONEST

*Our lives improve only when we take chances and the first and most difficult risk we can take is to be honest with ourselves.*
WALTER ANDERSON, PAINTER AND WRITER

It sounds so simple, but it requires you to be honest not just with other people but also yourself. Let's take 'you' to start with. It requires you to be able to look in the mirror, to reflect and to be true to yourself. If you've said you'll do something, to hold yourself accountable and follow through. It requires you to own up when you get something wrong.

When it comes to others, I want to quash a myth that originates from the 'I'm so honest club'. You know the ones… they're the sort who say, 'Oh yeah, I'm just so honest – I have to tell people exactly what I think.'

Sorry, that's not honesty. That's stupidity served with a lack of emotional intelligence and a large helping of arrogance.

Being honest with others is as much about acting with warmth and kindness as it is about telling them the truth. But being honest with others is key.

## TAKE ACTION

*Most people live and die with their music*
*still un-played. They never dare to try.*
MARY KAY ASH, ENTREPRENEUR

Most people never dare because they worry that their idea is not perfect, that the timing is not good, that something may go wrong.

Well, the chances are that your idea is not perfect, that the timing is not good and that something will go wrong!

But come on. Give it a go. If not, you'll just end up looking back wishing you had.

And this is where the naked piece comes in. It's about being brave, being courageous. It's about being scared but giving it a go anyway.

## TAKE RISKS

*People who don't take risks generally make*
*about two big mistakes a year. People who do take*
*risks generally make about two big mistakes a year.*
PETER DRUCKER, CONSULTANT, EDUCATOR AND AUTHOR

To grow, we need to experience challenge. Therefore the ability or willingness to take risks – calculated risks – is an important element for everyone, and, being successful in any pursuit will require us to take risks. The GO NAKED approach to 'Agreeing Goals' provides a structure via which you can approach goals and thus mitigate certain risks – after all, it really comes down to the relative likely benefits versus the relative likely risks, and then having a plan.

However, as with the previous element, 'to take action', 'taking risks' is about giving it a go even when you're scared. Plus, the chances are that the biggest barriers are in your own mind rather than out there in reality.

## ASK FOR HELP

*The strong individual is the one who asks for help when he needs it.*
**RONA BARRETT, WRITER AND BUSINESSWOMAN**

We live in a world which encourages self-sufficiency rather than asking others for help, but don't try to do it alone. The chances are that you'll be far more successful, far quicker and have greater enjoyment if you ask other people for their help. Again, this takes bravery – bravery to put yourself out there and ask someone for help; bravery to share your idea; bravery to say 'I don't know'; and bravery to verbalise your goals.

But that's ok, because we need to be brave. And it's amazing just how powerful a tool it can be to ask someone else for help. They will rarely decline and the benefits can be huge.

# DON'T FEAR REJECTION

*A rejection is nothing more than a*
*necessary step in the pursuit of success.*
BO BENNETT, BUSINESSWOMAN

We fear, sometimes more than anything else, losing approval from others. The fear of rejection is widespread and dates back to tribal times, when being ejected from the safety of a group could have meant death. However, that's unlikely to be the case today. Therefore fear is more a result of our human conditioning and exists firmly in the mind rather than in reality. Remove fear and remove the largest barrier.

Rejection, in truth, is just a normal step along the way and one that we can either accept, embrace and learn from, or not. It can help us learn and help us grow. It allows us to find a better way. But in not accepting these things we reduce the likelihood of a positive reaction which could lead to further success.

# SHOW HUMILITY

*Drop the idea that you are Atlas carrying the*
*world on your shoulders. The world would go on*
*even without you. Don't take yourself so seriously.*
NORMAN VINCENT PEALE, MINISTER AND AUTHOR

Showing your humility makes you more credible and more believable. By remaining humble, you are receptive to opportunities to improve and it is those opportunities which can ultimately lead to success.

To be humble requires us to drop our mask.

Seeing humility in another is a beautiful trait. Some of the most successful people I know have this in abundance; some of the most successful people I know have this in zero capacity! So humility is not a measure of success, nor is it likely to be the primary driver of success. But it is a measure and driver of attractiveness.

Think about who you would be most drawn to, most attracted to and most inspired by. The person who parades everything they know or the person who knows not to parade?

## BE VULNERABLE

*Vulnerability is the birthplace of innovation, creativity and change.*
BRENÉ BROWN, SCHOLAR, AUTHOR AND PUBLIC SPEAKER

The thought of being vulnerable is in itself a scary place. If the mere sound of the word makes you feel uncomfortable, you're not alone. I'm there with you and I understand. But the reality is that we have to push past that feeling which, in truth, is just a sense associated with our own limiting beliefs. If we can embrace it and push past it, there is so much more opportunity out there.

Those who associate vulnerability with weakness are mistaken and it's driven by their own fear. Fear of what others may think and fear of what understanding where that fear comes from may reveal.

But that's ok. It's normal. It's just time to accept that we have to embrace that feeling and understand the relationship between our comfort zone and safety zone. As Seth Godin describes beautifully in his book, *The Icarus Deception*:

> *The safety zone has changed, but your comfort zone has not. Those places that felt safe – the corner office, the famous college, the secure job – aren't. You're holding back, betting a return to normal, but in the new normal, your resistance to change is no longer helpful.*

Being naked, being vulnerable really means to re-align your comfort zone with the new safety zone and to do so is going to feel uncomfortable. It's going to feel risky and you're going to feel exposed. However, if you want to grow, develop and be successful, there is no other viable or sustainable alternative.

All the elements I have described above can contribute to being naked – to be authentic, to be honest, to take action, to take risks, to ask for help, to not fear rejection, to show humility and, at the core, to live with vulnerability.

So as you reflect on the different principles of GO NAKED, keep this sense of living with vulnerability at the forefront of your mind. As you work through each of these principles, consider how you do so with a sense of vulnerability, as to live with vulnerability is not a sign of weaknesses but a sign of great inner strength, awareness and confidence.

# GO NAKED TODAY

*The path to success is to take massive, determined action.*
ANTHONY ROBBINS, COACH, AUTHOR AND SPEAKER

The principles we have reviewed in *GO NAKED* represent not a cyclical or linear approach, but one which is a matrix of over-lapping and inter-connecting elements. Each, to some degree, has an influence on the others and in order to get the most out of them, we have to approach all of them with the right mind-set – a mindset of nakedness.

There is nothing groundbreaking in the theory here – it's really quite simple and that's the beauty of it. The whole premise of *GO NAKED* is that we can step away from the majority and develop stronger, more successful relationships by adopting an approach which is more authentic, more real; which strips away the unnecessary layers, and then focuses on how to add greater significance to others. By following these principles, we *can* step away from the majority.

The extent to which we are successful will, in most instances, be determined by the number of people we build quality rela-tionships with. This cuts across all aspects of life, both busi-ness and personal. Whilst the initial idea was focused on those in professional selling roles, the principles are transferable to wherever there is the need to communicate and influence to build great relationships.

However, we have to take action. We have to take what we see here as being those determining elements of success and apply them. Apply them immediately, apply them today, bit-by-bit, until this becomes ingrained in our approach and an unconscious competence. In other words, something that we do in the right way, at the right time, automatically.

The principles described here are not for a minority or an exclusive few, but available for all of us who want to positively develop the way in which we interact with others. You don't have to wait to be chosen. You have to step forward and take action.

An important point within the seven principles of GO NAKED is that there needs to be a balance across all steps. Doing one or two of the steps brilliantly is a great start, but in order to get the most out of your relationships then they all need attention and development. It would be easy to focus on the area in which you already succeed or believe you are strongest, but in doing so you would limit your potential.

The other point here is that there are a lot of common themes which cut across all the steps. For example, to Get Genuinely Curious requires the development of your emotional intelligence, your ability to Notice and Manage Yourself and Others. To Keep Adding Value you need to be able to challenge others and so you need to be able to further demonstrate empathy. In order to achieve your goals, Agree Goals and support the achievement of other people's goals then you need to Do It and Deliver on your promises – and vice versa. And in Embodying Enthusiasm we can add value and help support goal development, but it needs to be done at the right time and in the right way – which is emotional intelligence.

Some of the elements within *GO NAKED* may resonate with you more than others. Some may validate what you already do while others may make you feel uncomfortable. Keep in mind that as we venture into discomfort, we increase our comfort zone – and so the next time we go that way it will be far easier. As our comfort zone increases, so do the experiences and opportunities that we will open our minds to.

The opposite is also true, that in not taking these steps and feeling uncomfortable, our comfort zone decreases. We become more risk averse, less open to change, opportunities and new experiences. We stop trying new things, stick to what we know and shelter within the confines of our comfort zone. There's no right or wrong here and it's entirely up to you – but give some thought to which is the more positive approach to take.

Let me finish by saying that life is a contact sport, business is a contact sport and ultimately it is people and the way in which we interact with people that will make the difference. That is what we need to focus on and to remove the learned behaviours which are inhibiting our growth, development and greater success.

If we focus on the mindset and principals of *GO NAKED*, I believe we can all build stronger relationships and achieve greater success together.

*To live with vulnerability*

*Be authentic*

*Be honest*

*Take action*

*Take risks*

*Ask for help*

*Don't fear rejection*

*And show humility*


*Let this become a way of life*

*To communicate, to influence*
*and to build great relationships*

*Get Genuinely Curious*

*Offer Something Different*

*Notice and Manage Yourself and Others*

*Agree Goals*

*Keep Adding Value*

*Embody Enthusiasm and*

*Do It And Deliver*


GO NAKED.

# ACKNOWLEDGEMENTS

Whilst writing a book is undoubtedly a time consuming project it has also been a thoroughly enjoyable one which I hope to repeat. The inspiration and content of this book has been gained over many years and from various sources who have shaped my ideas and thinking about business, selling and relationships. Any success I have enjoyed to date or will do in the future has been largely as a result of those people, without whom neither my career nor this book would have developed.

It would be difficult if not impossible to acknowledge all of those people but I'd like to mention a few who have been and continue to be instrumental.

Caroline Redmond, Les Davies, Bob Brooks, Lorraine Walker-Smith and Lesley McCabe from Vygon UK, who gave me my first job and with it an education in business values. Ian Newell, Ashley Wells and Chris Norman from DePuy, who opened out my thinking and supported my personal development. Raphael Pasacud, Richard Twomey and Claudia Gallo from Align Technology who gave me a wonderful opportunity which was everything I wanted.

I'd also like to thank Barry Buckley, Michelle Lally, Andrew Holliday, Sheldon Krancher and Isaiah Hankel, who allowed me to tell their stories; to Alison Hardingham who changed my life; and Parminder Basran who continues to help me aim higher.

Grateful thanks also go to Jacqueline Biggs who has helped enormously and allowed me to learn from her experience, whilst Shaa Wasmund, Jamie Smart and Michael and Christine Heppell all provided words of guidance and support along the way.

I've long enjoyed reading books on business and personal development, but those which really made a difference were by Patrick Lencioni, Seth Godin, Tim Ferris, Shawn Achor, and Simon Sinek. My grateful thanks go to these pioneers.

Also, John Montgomery at Blue Sky Information Design, Rebecca Philpott from The DesignPot and Lucy McCarraher and the team at Rethink Press who have also helped greatly in bringing this project together.

Finally, special thanks go to my wonderful parents who gave me everything and continue to do so; my two boys who make me smile every time I see them; and my beautiful wife Andrea who is easily the most remarkable person I've met, who provides unwavering support and embodies the principles in this book.

# THE AUTHOR

Michael believes that strong relationships and connections lead to success and that the best way to create them is to 'GO NAKED'.

Michael graduated from the University of Leeds after completing a BSc in Medical Biochemistry. After taking up a sales role in a medical device company, he quickly established a successful career in the industry, which saw him appointed to numerous sales and marketing management roles across three multi-national companies, most recently as Director of Sales for Europe.

In 2010, Michael was awarded an MBA with distinction from the University of Warwick where his final dissertation focused on strategies for market entry. In 2012, Michael completed his Professional Certificate in Coaching at Henley Business School.

In 2013 Michael created GO NAKED® – a series of training, coaching and development programmes based on seven principles of success which can help individuals and businesses to increased performance. He now works as a Coach, Speaker and Advisor.

If you think Michael could help you or your business you can contact him directly via:

**Email:** michael@gonakedselling.com
**Twitter:** @smith_michaelj
**Facebook:** www.facebook.com/gonakedselling

You can also read his weekly blog at www.gonakedselling.com

Lightning Source UK Ltd.
Milton Keynes UK
UKOW04f1540270314

228953UK00002B/3/P